Do You Web 2.0?

CHANDOS
INTERNET SERIES

Chandos' new series of books are aimed at all those individuals interested in the internet. They have been specially commissioned to provide the reader with an authoritative view of current thinking. If you would like a full listing of current and forthcoming titles, please visit our website www.chandospublishing.com or e-mail info@chandospublishing.com or telephone number +44 (0) 1223 499140.

New authors: we are always pleased to receive ideas for new titles; if you would like to write a book for Chandos, please contact Dr Glyn Jones on e-mail gjones@chandospublishing.com or telephone number +44 (0) 1993 848726.

Bulk orders: some organisations buy a number of copies of our books. If you are interested in doing this, we would be pleased to discuss a discount. Please e-mail info@chandospublishing.com or telephone number +44 (0) 1223 499140.

Do You Web 2.0?

Public libraries and social networking

LINDA BERUBE

CHANDOS
PUBLISHING

Oxford   Cambridge   New Delhi

Chandos Publishing
TBAC Business Centre
Avenue 4
Station Lane
Witney
Oxford OX28 4BN
UK
Tel: +44 (0) 1993 848726
E-mail: info@chandospublishing.com
www.chandospublishing.com

Chandos Publishing is an imprint of Woodhead Publishing Limited

Woodhead Publishing Limited
80 High Street
Sawston
Cambridge CB22 3HJ
UK
Tel: +44 (0) 1223 499140
Fax: +44 (0) 1223 832819
www.woodheadpublishing.com

First published in 2011

ISBN: 978 1 84334 436 0

© Linda Berube, 2011

British Library Cataloguing-in-Publication Data.
A catalogue record for this book is available from the British Library.

Typeset in the UK by Concerto.
Printed in the UK and USA.

Contents

List of figures

List of acronyms

BFW	big frickin' wall
ILS	integrated library system
IM	instant messaging
IT	information technology
MMORPG	massively multiplayer online role-playing game
OPAC	Online Public Access Catalog
ROI	return on investment
ROR	rate of return
RSS	Really Simple Syndication
SL	Second Life
SOPAC	Social Online Public Access Catalog
SROI	Social Return on Investment
UKOLN	UK Office for Library and Information Networking

About the author

Linda Berube's career has been defined by change: initiating it, driving it and managing the risks and anxieties associated with it. This has been true of every position she has held, including management and development roles with regional, national and international partnerships in the USA and UK. Her experience lies in creating and managing services, some successful and some not, using new technologies, beginning with UK national demonstrator services delivered through EARL, a national networking consortium, at a time when almost no libraries or government offices even had websites, and culminating most notably with the People's Network Enquire service, which at one time included the participation of almost two-thirds of English public library authorities. Much of her career in technology and service development for public libraries in the UK has been about driving changes which support increased interactivity with users.

She has a considerable list of publications and presentations on topics including analysis of library cooperation, the digital divide and technology forecasting, as well as consideration of the societal, government and private sector context for technology take-up. She has advised on a number of central government strategies, policies and initiatives for such stakeholders as the DCMS (Department for Culture, Media and Sport), the MLA (Museums, Libraries and Archives Council), Becta (British Education and Communications Technology Agency) and JISC (Joint Information Systems Committee). The British Council in Romania retained her as a consultant for marketing electronic resources, and she was part of a multinational delegation to Russia, participating in a UNESCO World Information Society conference and state visits to archives and museums.

Currently, as a consultant manager, she coordinates policy, research and project work for the Legal Deposit Advisory Panel, a UK non-departmental government body charged by the government with making recommendations on regulations for the legal deposit of digital resources. She works closely with national libraries, publishing trade associations, online and print publishers, scholars and researchers, as well as copyright and licensing experts. In addition to her work with the panel, she advises a number of public sector organisations in the implementation of new technology, including blogs and social networking services, and provides clients with reviews and forecasts on the technology landscape, present and future – an example of which, 'On the road again – the next e-innovations for public libraries', was commissioned by the LASER Foundation (2005).

Acknowledgements

In addition to the inspiration and knowledge derived from the many references listed at the end of the book, I am also indebted to the following people for their advice and permission to use the images in the book.

Susan Allen, director of technology services, Worthington Libraries, Worthington, OH, USA.

Ian Baaske, developer, North Suburban Library System, Wheeling, IL, USA.

Andy Baker, library hub manager, Bedfordshire County Council, UK.

John Blyberg, assistant director for innovation and UX, Darien Library, Darien, CT, USA.

Cali Bush, director of legal services, O'Reilly Media Inc., Sebastopol, CA, USA.

Kyle Cook, web education and outreach, Nashville Public Library, Nashville, TX, USA.

Hypatia Dejavu, Community Virtual Library on Second Life.

Kimber Fender, director, Public Library of Cincinnati and Hamilton County, Cincinnati, OH, USA.

Elaine Fulton, director, Scottish Library and Information Council/CILIP in Scotland, Hamilton, UK.

Patricia Garret, People's Network librarian, Portsmouth City Council Library Service, Portsmouth, UK.

Frances Hendrix, former secretary, LASER Foundation.

Joanne John, application support consultant and enquiry administrator, OCLC, Birmingham, UK.

Anne Kozak, library director, Thomas Ford Memorial Library, Western Springs, IL, USA.

Debbie Mynott, manager, Stories from the Web, Birmingham Library, Birmingham, UK.

Eli Neiburger, associate director for IT and production, Ann Arbor District Library, Ann Arbor, MI, USA.

Rachel Peacock, reference and information manager, Gateshead Libraries and Arts Service, Gateshead, UK.

Denise Raleigh, director of marketing, development, and communications, Gail Borden Public Library District, Elgin, IL, USA.

Gail Richardson, manager online services, Oakville Public Library, Oakville, ON, Canada.

James Smith, electronic information librarian, City Library and Arts Centre, Sunderland, UK.

Ann Marie Wieland, Archives, Cleveland Public Library, Cleveland, OH, USA.

Doreen Williams, Stories from the Web, Birmingham Library, Birmingham, UK.

Prologue

'Maybe what we are going to learn out of this isn't some technological thing,' Farah said. 'Maybe what we're learning is to be more comfortable with a higher level of risk.' I asked if he did feel comfortable with the risks the program was taking. He thought for a moment. 'I realize there's no other way to do it, so I am comfortable with it.' (Rauch, 2008)[1]

Do you Web 2.0? A confession

The most critical issue for public librarians today is bringing their services out of the dark of the hidden web, and in so doing creating a new role for themselves in the digital community. Accomplishing these goals requires commitment to evolving an already strong local and cultural brand to one equally strong in the web environment. They do not necessarily have to choose between a web and a physical space (although it sometimes feels like it, given budget considerations), but if they really want to reach a wider audience, to achieve relevance beyond a few already dedicated online library users, to ensure as much as possible a future, then they really have to address this challenge.

That this is *the* issue is contentious, I know. However, it is essentially the issue for all public-facing services, be they in the commercial or public sectors, and especially those rooted to a physical space and not 'born digital'. Consider clothing and book stores: their entire business, service and delivery models were based solely on customers coming into shops to purchase goods. Now, some businesses have had to make the tough choice between the physical and online spaces. This decision has required not only a change in business models, but in service and delivery models. And while business models may differ, there is a similar sort of pressure on the public library service and delivery model.

I know there are a few who would disagree that the digital environment poses the most significant challenge, but then again there are probably a few who would think 'sounds about right, that's why we are into Web 2.0 now instead of later'. I can see both sides, having worked in public libraries in both the USA and the UK. And I understand the concern about taking risks, especially in a public sector environment. In fact, before we proceed, I have a confession of sorts.

Back in 2000, when I was managing research and online services for a UK national public library networking consortium, I received an e-mail from a company in the USA that produced commercial chat software. This company, whose software was already used by a number of libraries in the United States, was trying to set up a demo of chat at a conference in London, and it wanted the involvement of our national Ask A Librarian service, then using web-form software – an asynchronous service. At the time I was not entirely sold on the merits of chat-based reference, and as it happened the public library networking consortium was closing up shop. I was in the middle of finding homes for the online services and really couldn't spare the time, nor ask the librarians to give time to such an endeavour.

Fast forward to 2003: I am now managing a regional partnership, and have successfully transferred the administration for the national service to the portfolio of services managed by the partnership. I am looking at ways to grow the service, bring it up to date a bit. We do a pilot, talk to a few people in high places, get some seed funding – and web-form Ask A Librarian becomes in 2005 chat-based People's Network Enquire.

The point of the story is that, as a working librarian, I wouldn't really class myself as an 'early adopter', one of those people who have to try immediately every new technology available. I realise that the 'diffusion of innovations' theory (Rogers, 2003) crops up frequently in discussion of libraries and Web 2.0. But I suppose it is one of those things like Web 2.0: it seems to be describing something after the fact. We all know the librarians who are in a mad rush to try everything, classed by Rogers in the theory as the innovators and early adopters. And so it goes through the scale of implementation, right down to the laggards, which seems a rather harsh term to me, but I am sure it is being used in only the most scientific and research-oriented way. In 1995, when I was working in an American public library, staff tried to interest me in the internet when it was still all gopher and Jughead and Veronica, but I didn't want to know as I thought there must be an easier way (or maybe I was just being a laggard). So I was one of those sheep only lured on to the internet by the bright colours and graphics of the World Wide Web. But by 1996 I had designed my first webpage, writing the HTML code myself, in the UK. My only foray into early adoption has been with the Blackberry Storm, and although it's still early days for Blackberry and this technology, I wonder quite frequently why I have broken the habit of a lifetime.

Oddly enough, though, my career in the UK has been all about trying to persuade public libraries, through the safety net of collaboration, to try new technologies. Still, I am innately sympathetic to those who hang back and adopt a wait-and-see attitude. And although there are plenty of early adopters who have taken to Web 2.0, a few of whom are featured in this book, there are still probably more libraries hanging back to see what happens.

About the book

In a sense, this book is for both sets of librarians. For the early adopters who perhaps are not getting the flood of responses they thought mere implementation might provide, there is an opportunity to consider how really to transform libraries *and* library service. And for the not-so-early adopters, concerned about risks and capacity, there are some excellent examples which allow for a more incremental approach. Real Web 2.0 implementation is quite a bit different than anything that's gone before, e-mail, webpages and catalogues on the web notwithstanding. Just as being on the web changed the shape and range of library services, Web 2.0 may determine the library's relevance to web communities.

This range of issues – how to approach Web 2.0 given relative capacities, how to build communities, how to raise the public library profile – is explored in this book through consideration of the current use of Web 2.0 tools in public libraries, especially as part of a process that opens them up to the kind of social networking that can lead to the 'co-created' library. The book covers a number of topics.

Are libraries ready?

Although the level of interaction with users through Web 2.0 tools is different from changes to service in the past, public libraries are no strangers to the disruptions of technology. The book begins by considering a few such changes, and whether implementation 'by increment' or 'by revolution' will be necessary to respond to the demands of social networking.

A consideration of what it means to Web 2.0

No self-respecting book about Web 2.0 could begin without an attempt to reconcile the various definitions of it and, to some degree, Library 2.0. In Chapter 2 the emphasis will not be so much on the technical side – although we will look at Web 2.0 from the perspective of levels of network functionality, as laid out by Web 2.0 guru Tim O'Reilly – but more on the perspective of the social ethos, 'hive mind' or 'wisdom of the crowd' advocated by such experts as Charles Leadbeater. These experts are on the whole a bit exacting when it comes to Web 2.0 implementation. However, in their own way, they outline the incremental and revolutionary levels which may help libraries to assess their readiness to embrace the full functionality of the technology and what it entails, to decide at what level to begin implementation or to review how effective their current Web 2.0 initiatives are.

A review of a range of Web 2.0 tools

Chapter 3 reviews the available techniques, and at the same time looks at a host of examples of libraries just getting on with doing it. When I read professional literature, I look first for the front-line examples: to get a little inspiration, to learn some lessons and, most importantly, to collect contacts to consult when I want to try out some new technology. This chapter is not so much a guide for how to use each tool, rather it is a collection of examples of implementation for public service. I have spent a considerable amount of time searching out library Web 2.0 services and testing them from a user perspective. While not conducted according to the strictest research procedure, my research has resulted in certain observations and impressions which in some cases are quite similar to those formed by the first-time non-librarian user. It is often that first impression, and how many users share it, that makes or breaks a service. Where possible, I will look at the nature of the implementation: are libraries using the Web 2.0 tools but in a Web 1.0 way, or are they really reaching out to open communication with their communities?

Although the book's title refers to social networking, which would imply services such as Facebook, many Web 2.0 tools are used to facilitate sociability on their own or incorporated into social network services, and so are included in the book. Although it is a book about Web 2.0, the point here is that it is not the technology but how it is being used. So a range of Web 2.0 tools is considered, as well as Web 1.0 tools, all from the perspective of social interaction and how they can be used to build or attract communities – the important participation framework to develop content or simply just to communicate.

The progress of UK public libraries on the web, from flat HTML pages to user-created services

I'm a firm believer in the 'not knowing where you are going if you don't know where you have been' philosophy, especially as it relates to service development. UK public libraries and their technological evolution over the past ten years serve as an interesting overall case study for the mixture of incremental and revolutionary changes which have propelled libraries forward. In Chapter 4 we will follow this progress and look at specific library implementation in more depth, through case studies, than the examples offered in the web tools chapter. In that chapter the approach is more from a user's perspective, whereas in this chapter librarians' experience with the new technology is represented and analysed.

The business case for Web 2.0

Whether a library works to make small or major changes, preparation is key. Previous chapters have demonstrated that implementing this technology is the easy part (except, of course, if an IT department expressly forbids it). Addressing legal, corporate and other risk issues has the potential to stall a new service. Most of all, establishing the participation framework and properly branding the service to attract users, new and old, will be the ultimate mark of success and the most challenging of all. Doing the research, understanding and addressing these issues, putting together the business case, should go a long way to minimising risk and maximising success. The business case is not just an advocacy document: it should help a library better understand its own motivations and objectives, an important critical success factor.

Everyone is on the lookout for that magical 'business case', the one format that can satisfy the advocacy requirements for a range of stakeholders. That business case is not to be found in this book, and I would challenge anyone to find it in any book; rather, this book includes areas common to a number of business case formats. What is important is collecting the requisite evidence and the champions, and, above all, identifying the practicable objectives for success. Even if a library starts with a small service, targeted at a restricted number in the community, done well this service can provide the base or pilot for those gradual improvements that catapult the library over the big wall that prevents significant change (as described by Kathy Sierra in Chapter 1). It is not unusual to underestimate the impact a new technology can have not only on traditional service delivery, but on staff capacity and confidence. Small, targeted pilots are an important part of a persuasive business case and also prepare staff for the possible radical change to come.

The observations and conclusions drawn in the above-mentioned areas are the result of a qualitative research methodology of sorts which involved many hours of looking at hundreds of websites, at first as a casual user and then with the object of evaluating such issues as visibility on corporate sites, frequency of updates, frequency or level of interaction with users, numbers of fans, followers, etc., date last updated, length in operation, etc. The information for the case studies was gathered through interviews with librarians and using the sites according to these objectives. I maintained a log of sites visited and impressions gathered based on the use objectives, from which I have selected examples for the book.

About the readers of this book

The book can be used by library managers and front-line staff alike, particularly in public libraries which are looking to collaborate truly with their communities to create better, more efficient means of information exchange on the web, or even, if they are feeling particularly daring, to co-create the library.

Its message should also be considered by those at the national level, whether in professional organisations or in government, who are responsible for the future of public library service. The next few years will require some big, risky, long-range thinking, which involves not just understanding what teenagers are doing *now*, but what all age groups respond to now and in the future. This type of thinking and strategy might just propel public libraries over that big wall.

It is important to note that while the book is directed at public librarians, and uses both UK and North American public library implementation as its point of reference, the information herein is of use to all librarians looking to take on this new technology. In addition, the emphasis is on the creation of Web 2.0-based services to be used by the public, and the book addresses the issues related to public service development, not development of services for internal use, such as training or document writing. This is not to take away from some of the good work that has been done using Web 2.0 on the staff side. There has also been some excellent work in the UK and USA on local customisation of catalogues and design of websites. Many libraries have had knowledgeable technical staff in-house to implement and maintain these services, or have been lucky enough to import development from third parties. However, for most public libraries certainly, this type of expertise is costly and out of reach. While I refer to some of the notable examples in this area, it is worth mentioning that most of the examples are of libraries working with out-of-the-box type of tools: not highly customisable, but low-cost, accessible, not subject to local firewalls and easy to implement and use.

Notes

1. I hope readers will excuse quotes from General Motors staff regarding the development of their new hybrid car, the Volt. Quotes from the car industry might be a bit unfortunate in the current climate, but developing new products in a competitive environment is of some relevance.

Part I
Public libraries and social networking: can we Web 2.0?

1

Public libraries and digital climate change

His life's work: already to be some place else by the time anyone else got there. (Powers, 2002)

A sign of the times

This book, as is the way of most writing endeavours, began as one thing and became something else. In the initial drafting, it was intended as a straightforward introduction to Web 2.0 tools with examples of good practice, rounded off by some business case principles for local implementation. At its core, these are still the objectives.

However, over the period of time it has taken to write it, relentless changes in terms of widespread use of Web 2.0, and subsequent library interest, have occurred. For example, there was a social networking explosion provoked by micro-blogging. Twitter went from something navel-gazing celebrities and uber-geeks used to a communication network that inspired protest over the Iranian election (Schectman, 2009[1]) and provoked a freedom of speech and of the press debate in Britain (Booth, 2009).

In an instant what was once my introduction, an exhortation similar to that in other Web 2.0 articles and books, filled with all kinds of statistics reasoning why librarians needed to jump on the social networking bandwagon, how everyone is doing it, became passé. There is no longer any need to prove the number of young people involved in some kind of web-based activity: the message from every quarter seems to be that Twitter and those of its ilk are the 'it' tools, and libraries had better get in quickly, especially if they are to bag that elusive prize, the teenager.

The real revelation would be evidence of a backlash against some of the more negative aspects of socialising in this manner. While any major backlash is unlikely to happen in the near future, it seems that Fortune's wheel has turned, ever so slightly, for Twitter anyway, if the Morgan Stanley (2009) report, 'How teenagers consume media', is anything to go by. Based on input from a 'resident expert' – Matthew Robson, a 15-year-old summer intern – the report made newspapers with such headlines, for example from *Times Online*, as 'Twitter is for old people, work experience whiz kid tells bankers' (Pavia and Kishtwari, 2009). In the *Times* article, Robson elaborates: 'It's aimed at adults... Stephen Fry is not particularly cool. Also, for the cost of one tweet you could send quite a few text messages.'[2]

This and other research would suggest, firstly, the faddishness of these tools (anyone still using MySpace?), and that for different generations there are different interests and ways of communicating (nothing new there). According to Claire Cain Miller (2009) in the *New York Times*, it is largely a myth that teens drive the popularity of social technology: just 11 per cent of 12–17-year-olds use Twitter, 14 per cent use MySpace and 9 per cent Facebook. But, more importantly for libraries, hopes and services for attracting any audience should not be built around the technology alone, especially when one segment of that audience, teenagers, tends not to be loyal for long. Miller points to their use of social technology: teenagers were responsible for the initial growth of Friendster and MySpace, but then transferred their loyalty to other sites, Facebook among them. In a column for the British magazine *Prospect*, Tom Chatfield (2009), talking about the use of Nintendo game consoles to teach mathematics, observed 'Anyone who thinks of technology as a magic wand that can be waved to banish ignorance is sure to be sorely disappointed.'

Given these views, it did not seem quite enough to write a book that simply pointed librarians in the direction of Web 2.0. And, based on my review of libraries that have taken the plunge, not only did it appear that a good number had indeed expected the technology to be the magic wand, but they also seemed quite unaware of how to attract the attention of any users beyond those already dedicated to library service.

And it may be perfectly acceptable to want to attract only local users. However, a number of public libraries are using the technology in an attempt to reach out to non-users, teenage and otherwise. Or else why have Facebook, MySpace and Twitter pages? While the interest in new technology and taking library services to where potential new users are is a positive step towards change, believing that the technology itself will do the work of attracting new users is, if not a step backward, then a standing still which will certainly not strengthen the perception of public libraries within digital communities.

Whither libraries?

While Twitter (and Stephen Fry) may not lose any sleep over a summary dismissal from a teenager, Robson also has something further to say about use related to specific environments: 'Every teenager has some access to the internet, be it at school or home. Home use is mainly used for fun (such as social networking) whilst school (or library) use is for work' (Pavia and Kishtwari, 2009). This perception of libraries as having a specific function is borne out by other research. Librarians who think the mere implementation of technology can change this view, especially among teenagers and the older student population, should pay particular attention to a University of Michigan survey (Chapman, 2008):

> According to a recent study, 'a total of 23% of respondents stated that "yes" or "maybe" they would be interested in contacting a librarian via FaceBook and MySpace. Undergrads had a slightly higher than average percentage of 34%. Nearly half of the total respondents stated they would not be interested, but for various reasons – the biggest reason being that they feel the current methods (in person, email, IM) are more than sufficient. 14% said no because they felt it was inappropriate or that FaceBook/MySpace is a social tool, not a research tool.'

And from OCLC (2007):

> Almost 60 percent of those surveyed for an OCLC report 'Sharing, Privacy and Trust in our Networked World' said that building social sites was not the role of libraries. 'The library is there to be a place where you can borrow books and sometimes use computers, not for people's social lives,' said one UK 15-year-old.

I can see it from their perspective: just when they get themselves settled into a new hang-out online, here come the oldies, trying to sell them stuff or tell them about all the constructive things they should be doing with their free time. One can almost smell the desperation coming off some of the pages trying to be relevant to youth. This is not to discourage the use of social networking to connect with hard-to-reach members of the community: it has been interesting and heartening to see how readily libraries have taken to Twitter within a matter of months. Any web-based tool or service affords libraries a degree of editorial freedom, a freedom frowned upon behind the somewhat restricted comfort zone of local government firewalls. This is especially true for UK public libraries. Twitter has been easier to implement and maintain than any other social networking tool, including blogs. This enthusiasm bodes well for the profession, in that there is a contingent out there ready to take risks and even have a bit of fun with service delivery.

However, what the feedback from particularly savvy online users demonstrates is that services, whether Web 2.0 or other, need to have that perfect combination of well-defined brand, objective, community and participation framework, and method of delivery. What makes a service or brand relevant is not the technology; it is whether it is needed or desired by the community.

If the group they are trying so hard to attract perceives libraries in such specific terms, it is useful to consider, at both local and global levels, how much of a change to service and ethos libraries are willing to undertake to transform that image, and then to capture and keep the attention of the new users they may attract. Or is it necessary to change the image and the brand at all? Should we just enhance the strong brand we already have by creating new services using the new technology? The physical act of creating the Facebook page or the Twitter account is not the end of the process; it may be the beginning of a whole new way of delivering service and interacting with communities. This challenge could be an opportunity to strengthen an already strong brand.

And that brand can only be bolstered by preparation, firstly, for joining a new community, for make no mistake this is what using the new technology is all about: joining the digital community in a much more active way than simply setting up a website. Part of this preparation is the identification and articulation of role, objective, community, service and service delivery. Once these elements are well defined, technology for delivery can be decided upon and implemented. And it might be that this technology includes Web 2.0 tools. It will probably not consist solely of them, but the incorporation of these tools can be the first step in recognising the evolving nature of the interplay between communication and information. In the past, the mechanism – the book, the magazine – was narrowly defined, the communication going all one way, from author to reader. Now the communication is best represented by the London Tube map: around, up and down, across, sideways. The key is to explore and identify the new role of libraries in that exchange, and whether that new role requires a different kind of branding to promote libraries to the public.

We've been here before

A well-defined community, service and brand are critical, as, according to the Web 2.0 experts, there is no successful halfway implementation – either a library is prepared to take on user interaction and user-created content, or it is left behind using the software and services to perpetuate traditional, one-way communication with its community. Basically, the experts, as we will see in the next chapter, view web delivery in terms of step changes, and the full implementation of the Web 2.0 technology and ethos is the next logical and necessary step.

Libraries have faced challenges in the past which resulted in a significant shift in service delivery and ethos: automated and online catalogues, public service provision of computers and applications, followed by public provision for access to the internet[3] and the creation of their own webpages and online content, to name just three of the more disruptive. Because of two of these challenges, libraries firmly rooted in physical space, confined to the tyranny of geography (note how 'libraries' and 'librarians' are interchangeable, so identified are the people with the space), found themselves faced with the inevitability of the digital destination. However, social networking has the potential to transform libraries in a way that may be just as disruptive, just as radical, for it will usher in a level of user interaction not experienced before. The Web 2.0 tools which demand active social networking (and there are tools which allow for more passive use) invite the public to transform library spaces. Are librarians ready for this level of interaction?

There are some who think libraries, yes, public libraries, of all public sector departments, are usually the first to take on new technologies, and Web 2.0 tools will be no different: my experience working with service development in public libraries bears this out, as do the many excellent examples in the book.

However, for public libraries at least, the concerns about sustainability, capacity and marketing, combined with a risk-averse corporate culture, have meant that even when the new technologies are implemented this is done in a manner which is so restrictive and limiting that risk seems to play little part. And then the technology sits there, gathering dust, with neither the public nor librarians using it at all, never mind taking an interest in additional functionality. General Motors knows what is to be gained from risk:

> I think the whole company has now learned the lesson that when you set out and do bold things, you win, and when you're cautious and let someone else do the bold things, you lose. (Rauch, 2008)

Except, of course, when you set out to do the bold things and still lose. But that's the nature of risk when the stakes are high.

A perfect example of the library's chance at boldness was the online catalogue. It was pretty heady stuff, after getting over the somewhat revolutionary move of creating websites, to put the catalogue online as well as offering access to third-party commercial databases. Remember, getting rid of the card catalogue was akin to severing the umbilical cord that was the print-based inventory. And, for a time, libraries maintained both, one a kind of safety net constructed of pine. Whither the public library catalogue of today?

I have spent a good part of my career in the UK trying to make a network of distributed catalogues interoperate. The theory was that librarians and members of the public alike could search across and borrow from a number of catalogues, regardless of the local commercial library management system, without multiple search software. It didn't work, or rather the searching did, but only in the most rudimentary form, as the different versions of standards used by suppliers meant there were frequent problems with search results. Getting interlending systems to interoperate was only possible in test environments, and then not consistently. And at the time anyway there were too many obstacles, not all of them logistical, to home delivery across library authorities. So, well, no, it didn't work, but it points to the eternal struggle to unlock the library catalogue, not just from commercial restrictions but from the restrictions librarians themselves impose. For the most part, some pretty sophisticated middleware notwithstanding, catalogues remain the silos they were in pine cabinets. Librarians possess considerable data stores and high-functionality software, neither of which gets much of a workout.

After the success of getting catalogues and third-party database products on to their websites, not much more was done in the library sector to increase functionality and usability of these tools for library users. That's not to say that no thinking or effort was applied to the challenge: see Sarah Thomas's (2000) paper, 'The catalog as portal to the internet', for an example of the initial thinking on this subject.

No, it took the likes of Amazon and the Web 2.0 mash-up artists to unlock the traditional silos of book and other kinds of databases. Some would argue, and rightly so, that it is nowhere near any library's capacity, never mind a public library's, to effect that kind of change in the market, to influence the commercial software providers, or even develop products on its own. We tried to some extent in the regional partnership I managed, but faced too many insurmountable challenges. But while libraries were busy filling their technical specifications with more procedural and backroom functionality, others, like Amazon, took traditional library offerings to the next level of web development, and now libraries are copying them (the number of times I've heard references to the Amazon model at library conferences...).

There is a sense that this may also happen with Web 2.0 tools. While there are many good examples of libraries quick out of the starting blocks to implement RSS, blogs, micro-blogging and podcasts, it can be argued that not only is this implementation not as widespread nor as revolutionary as it should be, but it is also in danger of stagnating into the passivity of Web 1.0 functionality: used only to give information, to invite the odd comment or complaint, not much different from such asynchronous communication as e-mail. This type of static information delivery, about new books, services and events, is often defined by libraries as 'marketing'. Why, then, use technology that is clearly intended for building communities and facilitating communication and creativity among those communities? It could be argued that most of this use constitutes experimentation, a type of incremental application before taking on the full force of sociability demanded by these tools.

'By increment or revolution'

Kathy Sierra, a web developer specialising in user-based design and human behaviour in the digital environment, identifies what can be considered as the two approaches to development and implementation of any kind (Figure 1.1).

Sierra makes the choice plain, according to Darlene Fichter (2007a):

> The true art of product or service development might come down to this: Knowing when it's appropriate to make incremental

improvements and knowing when you need a revolutionary leap. However, she goes on to say that when organisations with similar products or services compete, the revolutionary improvement may be the only choice.

One view would suggest that public libraries are in that place: they are competing online for the attention of elusive user groups. And while there may be some very localised success stories among relatively small numbers within communities, taken all together they are not enough to create any large-scale change in perception about public library service delivery online. The following chapters will offer many useful examples of service delivery applied at the local level, involving either innovation achieved through incremental change or by breaking through Sierra's BFW (big frickin' wall), and by so doing inviting users to participate in what Fichter (ibid.) calls 'creating the library'. However, some of the examples will make clear how little an impact the magic wand of technology has made precisely because of the struggle with image, competing services and, most importantly, the motivation of users.

Knowing how to motivate users is critical for libraries wishing to take that next step in change of service online. However, this begs the equally important question of the motivation of libraries themselves. In the UK there is a struggle between the traditional (books) and the new (computers) that is played out periodically in the national press. I don't know whether to take heart from the continued, often emotional,

Figure 1.1　Incremental versus revolutionary improvements

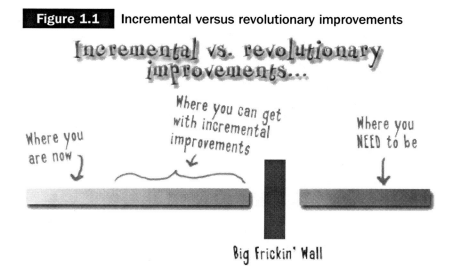

investment in public libraries, or be discouraged by the lack of awareness of one generation that might condemn libraries to irrelevance for another generation. So although I see why incremental change may be the only possibility for quite a few libraries, for a global rebranding or new brand a revolution may indeed be what is needed. UK public libraries have already experienced that revolutionary change in the form of the People's Network, a nationwide rollout from 2000 to 2003 of PCs and web content for public access. While there are those who still vigorously oppose the intrusion of computers in libraries, it intended and achieved the effect of enhancing the perception of online service delivery within library walls as well as without, across all UK libraries. Would this effect have been achieved as well and in as little time if libraries had been left to their own devices, budgets and timescales to install PCs and applications as well as create local content? If we consider the manner in which Web 2.0 services are developed currently, the answer would have to be no.

So, this book is a bit more than a look at Web 2.0 and libraries: it asks public librarians to consider that most critical issue identified in the Prologue, the public libraries' role online. If they do not want their services to remain hidden from the wider web community, and if this is truly the reason for experimenting with Web 2.0 technology, then libraries first must be clear regarding the intended purpose of this technology. There are plenty of genuine web gurus about – Fichter, Sierra and others to be discussed in the next chapter – who are quite specific about the purpose of products and services using Web 2.0 technologies. Service is the library's purpose ultimately; the technology supports the direction the service takes.

It is not overstating the case to say that all public libraries, and not just those in the UK, have been challenged by the web in an area they had considered their uncontested niche: information service and storage, free of charge. With the web, this niche has become overcrowded with all kinds of providers, and with the change in service and delivery models brought about in no small part by Web 2.0, the community of users libraries can claim as their own may shrink. Web 2.0 takes service provision to a different level – a level that is a sharp departure from the traditional public library method of operation.

In later chapters we will see the importance of determining corporate culture regarding change and the attendant risk brought on by new technology and greater participation. In the first instance, though, libraries must know what they are taking on with the new technology, and the (intended) purposes embraced not only by the commercial web but by the communities of the free web. And they must measure their motivation and capacity against the ultimate goal of social networking: the co-created web, and by extension the co-created library.

Notes

1. As this article suggests, the media reporting on Twitter was almost an event in itself. The article points out that Twitter's role might not have been as significant as described in other articles.
2. However, the wheel still appears to be turning. Recently, the Pew Internet & American Life Project (2009) revealed that, in the words of an Associated Press article (Irvine, 2009), 'Grudgingly, young people finally flock to Twitter.'
3. From my experience in public libraries in both the USA and the UK, for the USA these changes for the most part happened sequentially, while in the UK they happened at the same time as a consequence of the national initiative, the People's Network. For instance, at the Lawrence Public Library, at which I worked just before coming to the UK, computers for 'word processing' – in addition to typewriters – and the automated catalogue were provided for the public quite a while before dedicated terminals for internet access were installed.

2

Web 2.0 ethos: hive mind and the wisdom of the crowd

In the spirit of the digital age's gift economy, Adie gave his masterpiece away, free for the downloading. The cheaper the game, the more players it gathered. And the more players that played, the more ingenious the strategies. Strategies proliferated, each one a complex program in its own right. And the more unanticipated strategies that poured into his game, the closer Adie came to that sense of total liberty he hadn't felt since the age of eleven... (Powers, 2002)

While it might be safe to assume that everyone has heard about Web 2.0, judging from the range of implementation in public libraries, it is not safe to assume that everyone knows what it is, and whether they are actually participating in a social network of any kind. In this book I will look at a range of Web 2.0 tools, with the aim of understanding how they are used to fulfil social functions on their own or within the context of social networking sites.

To understand what social networking is, and to what extent individual libraries, or libraries as a whole, can participate, it is important to distinguish between the technology and what in society is driving the technology. There is a popular perception that a number of people, especially teenagers, spend hours on the web just aimlessly pursuing links, which has partially given rise to the ongoing discussion about purposeful use of technology, especially in the educational environment with children and teenagers.[1] This concept has a particular relevance for Web 2.0 tools, in the sense that there is a purpose to collaboration: users are not just passively taking in information published on the web; they actively seek out others and form communities around the creation of online content. Moreover, users are quite often motivated to seek others and collaborate for personal reasons.

To understand how Web 2.0 tools in particular facilitate this purposeful use, it is necessary to understand what Web 2.0 is. Definitions do not always help:

> Web 2.0 is a living term describing changing trends in the use of World Wide Web technology and web design that aims to enhance creativity, information sharing, collaboration and functionality of the web. Web 2.0 concepts have led to the development and evolution of web-based communities and its hosted services, such as social-networking sites, video sharing sites, wikis, blogs, and folksonomies.

This definition from Wikipedia, found in 2008, is pretty specific about the applications, such as wikis and blogs, but what goes before that is a bit vague: 'living term', 'changing trends', 'Web 2.0 concepts'? So does that make the examples of tools listed at the end just a subset of Web 2.0, and not what is entirely meant by Web 2.0? And what is meant by 'concepts', and do they refer to 'changing trends' or 'technology and web design that aims to enhance creativity, information sharing, collaboration...'? I cannot be alone in finding this definition less than helpful.

Interestingly, when I went back to check on some of my original links, I found this change to the Wikipedia definition:

> The term 'Web 2.0' describes the changing trends in the use of World Wide Web (WWW) technology and web design that aim to enhance creativity, communications, secure information sharing, collaboration and functionality of the web. Web 2.0 concepts have led to the development and evolution of web-culture communities and hosted services, such as social-networking sites, video sharing sites, wikis, blogs, and folksonomies... Although the term suggests a new version of the World Wide Web, it does not refer to an update to any technical specifications, but rather to changes in the ways software developers and end-users utilize the Web.

Since the above change, the definition has in fact been altered yet again. I know these changes are a frequent occurrence on Wikipedia, but the rather lengthy history of changes for this concept emphasises the

Figure 2.1 Web 2.0 meme map

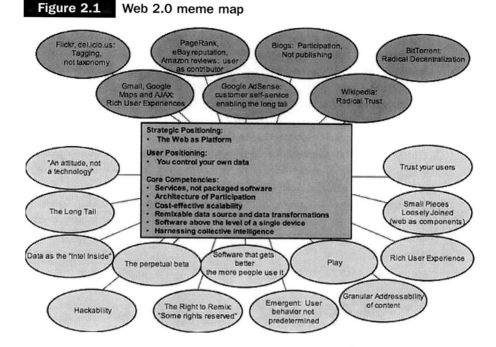

difficulty of defining it. Some may find the oft-reproduced Web 2.0 meme map (Figure 2.1) helpful, although if entirely unfamiliar with the concepts, it might cause even more confusion.[2]

These semantics make it difficult for those working on the ground, at least those librarians who are not also techies, to know if their libraries are wholly 2.0'd or not.

All of this semantic grappling, however, does not mean that there is a lack of basic concepts to help librarians to understand what Web 2.0 implementation really is. There are at least two requirements for Web 2.0 implementation, which appear in pretty much all of the discussions on definition. To a certain extent, a unique set of applications and tools define Web 2.0: Wikipedia itself is an example of the wiki, a web application that allows a number of users collaboratively to create content on the web. So implementing a number of applications like blogs, photo sharing and Facebook pages is basically what being a fully paid Web 2.0 community member is all about. Or is it?

Web 2.0 experts, Tim O'Reilly foremost as demonstrated by the meme map, insist that it is not just the applications, software or web design, but the ethos and environment in conjunction with the implementation –

essentially that part of the above definitions which refers not only to use, but purposeful use, and how it is different from what came before it: 'enhance[d] creativity, communications, secure information sharing, collaboration and functionality of the web'. First there is the communicating – gathering the crowd, building the hive (essentially developing the participation framework) – then the sharing, collaborating and creating. My initial reaction to the terms 'hive mind' and 'wisdom of the crowd' was diffident: at the extreme end, there are some fairly negative connotations attached, from mob rule to ideas, reports, etc. that experience 'death by committee'. The more positive implication is that some of the most democratic practices in the digital environment have the effect of leavening out the negative. And at their most basic level of meaning, this is what they refer to: creation based on a consensus. People can get riled up, and exchanges can be harsh, but the theory is that these occurrences will be or should be overridden by the democratic impulse.

Do you Web 1.0?

Public libraries know something about sharing information and about community. But this expertise has been challenging to translate from the physical to the digital setting. As will be discussed in Part III, public library websites have become increasingly sophisticated, but generally in providing directional information – times, addresses, in-house services, links and information provided by mostly commercial third parties. However, there are public librarians offering collaborative chat services, discussion boards, homework help online and online chat with authors and chief executives of local government alike. In other words, they have pushed the boundary of Web 1.0 technology. Of course, raising the spectre of Web 1.0 begs a definition. On this point, Wikipedia is a bit non-committal, saying that it is best understood in comparison to Web 2.0, and is a 'retronym'[3] for the web pre-dot.com (circa 2001) burst bubble.

Others, such as Jonathan Strickland, trying to describe Web 1.0 agree that quite a few of the tools or techniques considered to be Web 2.0 were available in one form or another pre-2001. According to Strickland (undated), Web 1.0 'sites are static; aren't interactive; and the applications proprietary'.

This definition essentially brings us back to purpose and use: Web 2.0 marks a departure of a kind because people are not just passively receiving or searching for information, but building, collaborating in a different way and using the tools to design and create. In the process they are creating their own tools, which they are willing to share with others for free (for instance, with open source software). In this sense, the technology has not really made the difference; the impulse to a free exchange of ideas and tools, through software, has made the difference. And according to Philip Rosedale, the founder of Second Life, while it is true that most people are happy to consume content, with such resources as Second Life people spend more time being creative; in fact, creativity becomes entertainment itself:

> We would look at the data and try to measure, 'what percentage of people's time are they spending creating versus consuming?' It was something like 30 percent creating and 70 percent consuming. We said to ourselves, 'well, surely as Second Life matures and a more normal mix of people, so to speak, are using it, that 30 percent is going to go down to one.' Because, that's what everybody says. In some sense, we'll know that the usage of Second Life is mature when that number has dropped to one. What we saw, then, over the last five years, was that the amount of time that people spent being creative really didn't drop very much at all. (Lamont, 2009)

Indeed, were the figure to drop, Rosedale would be more inclined to blame something in the Second Life software, something that might have made it too difficult to use, than to attribute it to a decrease in the interest in creating.

However, as Strickland (undated) points out, there are still uses for the somewhat passive exchange that describes Web 1.0. There are instances, especially in the case of local government and library websites, where static information is necessary and mandatory, and interactivity is not desirable. If Web 2.0 is the user-created web, then Web 1.0 is the information web, and there is still most decidedly a place for websites with static information. For libraries, the static aspects of their websites are important because they are still geographically based information-supply organisations. There are times when the wisdom of the crowd is not what is required; the wisdom or expertise of individuals or specialist organisations is what is necessary. Of course, they are also community, service and, some would say, educational organisations. In the digital environment it is this part of public libraries which could potentially benefit not just by using Web 2.0 tools, but in such a way that fosters and enhances community and creativity. In other words, libraries should look at a blending of the two approaches to web content and communication with their public.

Or do you Web 2.0? The sliding scale of implementation

I think this combination of approaches is truly a fundamental consideration for public libraries. The web, and the requirement for a web presence, has pushed them not only into an information creation role, but also competition with other kinds of information providers online. They had not faced this competition in their traditional services, and they were not required to create in quite the same way that the simple act of developing and maintaining a flat HTML website requires. Web 2.0 is calling on them to up their game by welcoming the creative contributions of their public. Because quite a few libraries using Web 2.0 tools have not moved away from an entirely Web 1.0 view, the technology does not have a positive impact on their services, and may even have a negative impact if it is creating more work and responsibility without a corresponding increase in use by the public.

This perspective leads to another way of looking at Web 2.0, what Tim O'Reilly (2006) calls a hierarchy of implementation: according to this view, there are four levels of implementation of Web 2.0 tools (presented by O'Reilly in descending order from most advanced to least), where only the highest level can be designated as truly Web 2.0. The determination is based entirely upon how the application is implemented. For example, at the highest level of Web 2.0 implementation, level 3:

> The application could ONLY exist on the net, and draws its essential power from the network and the connections it makes possible between people or applications. These are applications that harness network effects to get better the more people use them. EBay, craigslist, Wikipedia, del.icio.us, Skype (and yes, Dodgeball) meet this test. They are fundamentally driven by shared online activity. (Ibid.)

Levels 1 and 2 include applications which could exist successfully both online and offline, but to varying degrees. O'Reilly cites Flickr as an example of level 2 implementation because one could use photo management software offline. However, the unique success of Flickr is derived specifically from the functionality the internet offers:

> the online community, and the artifacts it creates (like the tag database) is central to what distinguishes Flickr from its offline counterparts. And its fuller embrace of the internet (for example, that the default state of uploaded photos is 'public') is what distinguishes it from its online predecessors. (Ibid.)

That this software is online, where it derives a considerable amount of additional functionality and global input, makes it much more than a photo management tool, whether it is used for individual or group purposes. Users are motivated to upload their photos not just for easy access and management but also to share and discuss them. Libraries have been attracted to Flickr and other photo-sharing sites like it, and point proudly to their photos as an example of Web 2.0 implementation. But it is important to note here that using Flickr does not by itself merit a level 2 ranking. Again, the type of use is important: that it is interactive and sustained, and that the advantage derived could not be gained by simply mounting photos on the library's corporate website or in the library itself. And, of course, it matters whose photos they are: if it's just library staff snapping away at each other and the public, there is hardly any user creation going on.

In the same sense does O'Reilly use Writely.com, now Google Documents, as an example of level 1 application, which includes desktop applications that are web-based. Wikis are open to global change and comment, whereas a tool like Google Documents offers a more controlled, closed environment where participation is only open to a small and restricted group of users. As with photo sharing, it comes down to how the network is exploited: Google Documents benefits from the network accrued to a closed membership, whereas a wiki leverages the functionality of a network to open participation to all.

Levels 0 and 1 differ only in the sense that level 0 applications really gain no additional creative functionality by being online: they may gain more in popularity and profile, and there may be more things that can be done online, but there is nothing added by exposing them to a community of users. O'Reilly points to MapQuest and Google Maps as examples because the data, which are the crucial feature, can be accessed as easily via cache.

Although O'Reilly's hierarchy has very much to do with how the network transforms applications, it is the functionality that provides opportunities for the creation and collaboration by communities that merits inclusion in the highest level of the hierarchy. It is not entirely a coincidence that those at level 0 are mostly based on datasets that users cannot alter in the same way that the content on Wikipedia, for instance, can be changed. So it is the network and software functionality of an application *and* creative collaboration that make a service thoroughly Web 2.0. Or, according to O'Reilly (ibid.), 'in the hierarchy of web 2.0 applications, the highest level is to embrace the network, to understand what creates network effects, and then to harness them in everything you do'.

While O'Reilly has focused on the harnessing of the network and its functionality as an enhancement to collaboration, Charlie Leadbeater (undated) distinguishes the level of Web 2.0 use not just by collaboration but by the *intention* to collaborate, which brings us back to motivation and purposeful use. The first 'level' is *indirect collaboration*, where the intention in using a website, or contributing to it, may be individual gain and consumption, while indirectly or even unintentionally supporting collaboration or a web community. Again, Flickr, or any photo-sharing site, is a useful example here, as many people, librarians included, contribute perhaps to communicate with families or raise the profile of an endeavour to local users. The fact is that data are still being contributed to the site, and the existing community can comment on these, or engage the contributor in other uses of the material, even if all this use is purely incidental. With *instrumental collaboration*, collaboration is exploited to achieve what might be intended as a specific, individual goal, but with the intention of leveraging a community to achieve it. Leadbeater cites the use of wikis and blogs, where the intention may be to write a book, for example, or plan, publicise or discuss events or performances. Leadbeater also identifies the creation of folksonomies as collaboration to achieve a very specific goal. Finally, there is *means/ends collaboration*, where collaboration is the goal. Leadbeater points out that some blogs are created just for this purpose: to discover a community of like-minded people, with no other goal or subject matter in mind. The most explicit example is social networking, where the express goal is reaching out, meeting, discussing, sharing ideas. In this sense:

there are two important by-products of means/ends collaboration 1.) shared value or meaning creation where understanding and knowledge are produced through social interaction – as in the physical world, social interaction shapes an individual's subjective perception. Examples of this include some aspects of folksonomies... 2.) social capital production – online networking sites have been shown to promote bridging and bonding ties between users. (Ibid.)

Here, Leadbeater echoes Rosedale's contention that sometimes creativity *is* the entertainment.

To Web 2.0 or Library 2.0?

It may be a bit of an afterthought at this juncture to mention Library 2.0, but if the discussion of the ever-changing definition of Web 2.0 confuses, then some of the thinking around Library 2.0, an offshoot, does as well. Wikipedia offers the following (although with a caveat about the quality of the definition):

> Library 2.0 is a loosely defined model for a modernized form of library service that reflects a transition within the library world in the way that services are delivered to users. The focus is on user-centered change and participation in the creation of content and community. The concept of Library 2.0 borrows from that of Business 2.0 and Web 2.0 and follows some of the same underlying philosophies. This includes online services like the use of OPAC [Online Public Access Catalog] systems and an increased flow of information from the user back to the library.
>
> With Library 2.0, library services are constantly updated and reevaluated to best serve library users. Library 2.0 also attempts to harness the library user in the design and implementation of library services by encouraging feedback and participation. Proponents of this concept, sometimes referred to as Radical Trust, expect that the Library 2.0 model for service will ultimately replace traditional, one-directional service offerings that have characterized libraries for centuries.

I have quoted this definition in full because a look at the discussion tab illustrates just how carefully wrought and contentious the end-product definition can be: what often detracts from the 'wisdom of the crowd' is that not-uncommon experience of how lifeless the written word can become once put through this wringer. It is interesting to note how far the semantic contentiousness for this definition extends. Concern is expressed that it appeared to have been designated for deletion, and possibly subsumed within the Web 2.0 definition. However, that consideration was dated 2006, and the definition, although there is still some dissatisfaction expressed with it, remains. One can't help but be amused by the inability of the hive mind/crowd wisdom to reach consensus on defining the very concepts that describe them. However, regardless of the jargon that has accumulated in this instance, there is some clarity here on how the social aspects of Web 2.0 can have an impact on the library processes, and even the library brand.

What I find more interesting than the actual definition of Library 2.0 is the concept of 'radical trust' and how that has contributed to the library application of Web 2.0. Radical trust implies something beyond the user-created web; indeed, it suggests a user-created library. Specifically, radical trust in libraries online would require the librarians to relinquish control to users or a community of users to create content on the corporate website. I think it is appropriate to let a librarian have the last word, not only to define Web 2.0, but to highlight the implications for libraries.

In her *Blog on the Side*, Darlene Fichter (2006, 2007b) reflects on the various influences on her thinking about radical trust, including Howard Rheingold, a writer on social media, and the public good in conjunction with the design of websites. Fichter believes, in much the same way that O'Reilly and Leadbeater do in their own spheres, that librarians and the communities they serve can be 'co-developers' of library services. Following on from this line of thinking, online library development is no longer database-driven (via electronic catalogues, indexes, abstracts and other reference works), in the sense of creating silos of static information, but more interactively service- and design-driven. In a sense, Fichter challenges librarians even more than O'Reilly and Leadbeater: it is easier to dismiss the Web 2.0 experts because they refer more to the web 'out there' – businesses, social networks, product development – places where Web 2.0 is supposed to have an impact, where they are supposed to be able to handle this kind of change more quickly. But when librarians start to envisage a radical rethink of the nature of libraries as they go about their business online, there is cause for concern and a question about whether librarians, and especially public librarians, can take on this challenge.

In considering the range of views on Web 2.0, especially the more philosophical aspect, librarians should understand the full implications of implementation: that the technology is the least of it, and while community-created content is the most of it, there is a very considerable point in between, as noted by Leadbeater – the purpose and motivation for building the community in the first place. In the following chapters we will explore how libraries have grappled with this issue, with relative degrees of success. For it is only in the understanding of both library and user motivation that success can be achieved.

Notes

1. Although 'purposeful use' may have different applications depending on the environment, essentially it refers to the use of technology according to certain objectives or goals, as in, for example, learning a new skill or creating content, such as a story, photograph etc.
2. The Web 2.0 meme map was 'developed at a brainstorming session during FOO Camp, a conference at O'Reilly Media' (O'Reilly, 2005).
3. Definition from Answers.com: 'A word or phrase created because an existing term that was once used alone needs to be distinguished from a term referring to a new development, as acoustic guitar in contrast to electric guitar or analog watch in contrast to digital watch.'

Part II
Web 2.0 tools and the librarians who love them: an overview

3

Do you Web 2.0? A round-up of Web 2.0 in public libraries

We can only build emergent systems if we have radical trust. With an emergent system, we build something without setting in stone what it will be or trying to control all that it will be. We allow and encourage participants to shape and sculpt and be co-creators of the system. We don't have a million customers/users/patrons... we have a million participants and co-creators. (Fichter, 2006)

Of course, behind all the various definitions of Web 2.0 are the tools themselves, each one challenging librarians to develop content and invite collaboration, whether in the form of an exchange of ideas or the creation of poetry, prose or audio and video recordings. These tools are what underpin that top level of Web 2.0 implementation in O'Reilly's hierarchy, combining all that is best in social and business networking to create and innovate. So although the title of this book refers to social networking, which may imply services or sites such as Facebook and Twitter, a range of Web 2.0 tools are reviewed in this and the next chapter (which also happens to include some Web 1.0 tools) from the perspective that all contribute to the 'socialness' and collaboration espoused by the Web 2.0 ethos.

Nothing dates a Web 2.0 book quicker than listing Web 2.0 tools. However, this is not a 'how-to' chapter; there are plenty of books and websites which recommend tools and give step-by-step help with implementing them, such as Phil Bradley's (2007) *How to Use Web 2.0 in Your Library*. This chapter is more of a 'some ideas for what might work best in my library' guide, including a number of library examples to provide inspiration and prompt implementation. These are examples which I have found in my own research, where I have predominantly played the role of user, spending many hours searching for and navigating around webpages, reviewing those I have found through my own discovery or the recommendations of others in blogs, articles or actual physical conversations. For this chapter, I felt very strongly that I wanted to approach the websites and services from a user's perspective, basing some of my analysis on those quick initial decisions users make about the quality of a website or service. So I purposefully have not spoken with the libraries involved in the following examples, and for this chapter at least (not so in the next chapter) I am not really interested in the lack of capacity, money or any of the reasons libraries offer to explain lack of success, maintenance or use. I am interested in the visibility of the sites to casual surfers as well as dedicated library users, how much care the owners take of them and what the response is from users, when that is possible to gauge – and it is more possible to gauge with Web 2.0-based services where the emphasis is on interaction. This is not formal research but first impressions, which are just as important on the web.

I suppose this sounds harsh, so I hasten to add that what I like about a number of the examples I have chosen is the effort by libraries to use the new technology to enhance traditional collections and services, for example print books and reader advisory. Far from dispatching reading and books to the tech-deprived hinterlands, the web has provided the space for communities of readers, who may or may not continue to meet in more traditional venues. Indeed, some exciting developments merge the real with the virtual environment, for example StoryTubes (see below), which combines book reports with YouTube. The significance is that the print book is still the 'killer app' but the sharing, communal aspect of reading is facilitated and supported by technology (Berube, 2005, 2006). That many of these examples are from US public libraries is not intentional, although these librarians have been among the first to experiment and sometimes create sustainable services. However, the uptake in the UK has increased significantly, I would say, within the last few years, as is demonstrated in this and the next chapter.

I have grouped these tools in what may appear to be an idiosyncratic manner. The organisation is reflective of the levels of implementation and involvement with the community, identified in the hierarchies presented in the previous chapter. The tools are arranged somewhat loosely according to the level of interaction at which librarians engage with their community, and to what extent they allow for user-generated content on their sites and in their services.

All the news that's fit to stream: RSS, blogs and podcasts

The library corporate site, that is to say its homepage, whether it be contained within a government site and server or part of a network of library sites and services, has traditionally combined static information with access to third-party commercial databases. To be sure, librarians often put together the information about services, locations and times themselves, but the content was and is mainly descriptive and directional and subject to infrequent change, especially when compared to commercial websites.

Web 2.0 tools such as RSS, audio and video podcasting, blogging and to a certain extent multimedia webcasting can assist librarians in extending this information beyond the corporate page, by delivering the information as and when it is updated directly to the e-mail accounts, personal webpages and mobile technology of those in local communities. They are all essentially communication tools; however, in the case of RSS and podcasts real-time communication with users is practically non-existent (although blogs can be attached to podcasts for an after-the-fact exchange). In that sense, they are asynchronous tools. Blogs and micro-blogs are communication tools which allow for more synchronous communication, although there is still the 'one-to-many' communication that differentiates them from truly collaborative services like wikis and social bookmarking.

This kind of Web 2.0 communication tool allows for the traditional way of delivering information – one way from librarian to user – but with more immediacy. This approach provides librarians with an opportunity to experiment with Web 2.0 software relatively risk-free, and to gain an understanding of how Web 2.0 can be integrated into library service. Once they overcome initial hesitations and potential obstacles, they can take the next step: actually entering the social network environment, using these and other tools with communities, collaborating on information delivery, essentially letting users disseminate information as well as create and promote services to other users.

Really Simple Syndication

Really Simple Syndication, or RSS, is a tool by which streams or feeds of information, such as news headlines, can be delivered to the public over a website or directly to e-mail or personal webpages. Many individual websites, for example blogs or news sites, offer RSS feeds of their content through a simple registration process. Or a number of different sources of information can be gathered and delivered on aggregator sites where users can pick and choose among multiple RSS feeds. RSS is one of the easiest tools for libraries to implement, as there is no cost and relatively little technical skill required. There are numerous services which provide an easy start-up. In fact, in his study of US public libraries and Web 2.0 implementation, Zeth Lietzau (2008) of the Colorado State Library observes that after online catalogues, RSS is among the group of Web 2.0 tools frequently implemented by 'early-adopter' libraries (see Prologue for an explanation of the diffusion of innovations theory). Such US public libraries as Cincinnati (Figure 3.1), Ann Arbor and Hennepin County offer an impressive array of feeds, especially pertaining to diverse reading subjects.

Data on the frequency of uptake for RSS feeds provided by libraries are hard to come by, perhaps because libraries are still, for the most part, in the early stages of live implementation.[1] And even though some librarians are becoming a bit more sophisticated in their use of RSS by linking feeds with other social networking services, such as Facebook, most of the information is traditionally one way. However, a delivery option that ensures an audience for the feeds is to move from the Web 1.0 mindset of one-way creation and delivery of information to the Web 2.0 ethos of the collaborative creation of information. This progression is accomplished by librarians and members of the community creating feeds together.

For example, book clubs or gaming clubs, with the help of librarians, could create webpages on the main library websites (or even Facebook pages) including calendars of events, meetings, related links and news which then can be transformed into feeds to which members and other users can subscribe. In this way, librarians provide key information, a site for groups and expertise, while the groups provide the additional interest in and traffic to library sites.

An example of combining RSS with community collaboration is NorthStarNet, an online community information network launched in 1995 by the North Suburban Library System in Illinois. Librarians helped community groups create homepages, using specially designed 'Community in a Box' software. Although NorthStarNet has now ceased operation, libraries are still using the community calendar (Figure 3.2), which groups can update themselves. Group members and those from

Figure 3.1 Cincinnati and Hamilton County Public Library

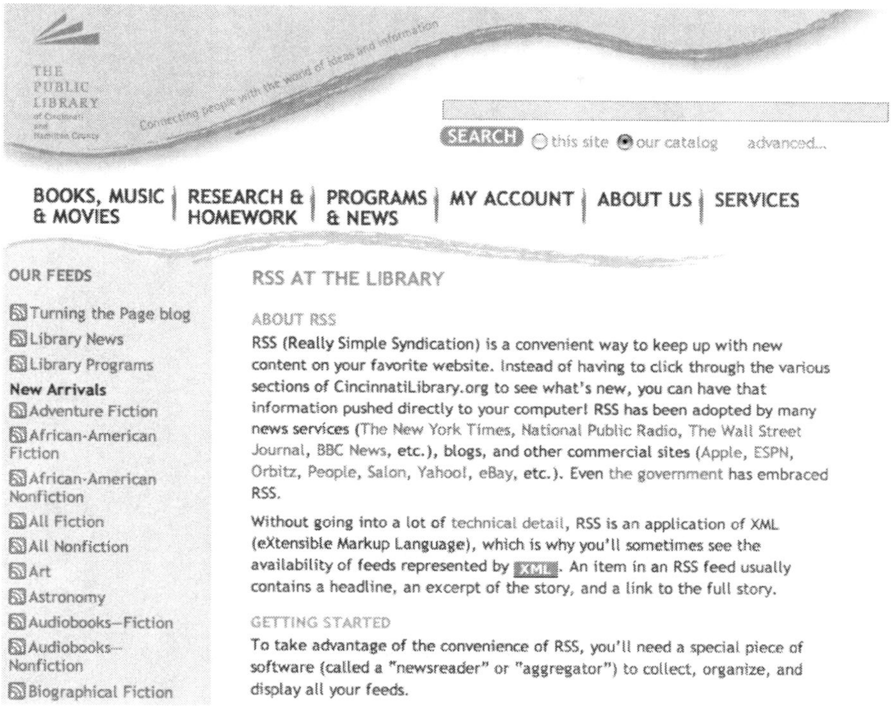

THE
PUBLIC
LIBRARY
of Cincinnati
and
Hamilton County

Connecting people with the world of ideas and information

SEARCH ◯ this site ◉ our catalog   advanced...

BOOKS, MUSIC | RESEARCH & | PROGRAMS | MY ACCOUNT | ABOUT US | SERVICES
& MOVIES | HOMEWORK | & NEWS

OUR FEEDS

🔊 Turning the Page blog
🔊 Library News
🔊 Library Programs
New Arrivals
🔊 Adventure Fiction
🔊 African-American
Fiction
🔊 African-American
Nonfiction
🔊 All Fiction
🔊 All Nonfiction
🔊 Art
🔊 Astronomy
🔊 Audiobooks—Fiction
🔊 Audiobooks—
Nonfiction
🔊 Biographical Fiction

RSS AT THE LIBRARY

ABOUT RSS

RSS (Really Simple Syndication) is a convenient way to keep up with new content on your favorite website. Instead of having to click through the various sections of CincinnatiLibrary.org to see what's new, you can have that information pushed directly to your computer! RSS has been adopted by many news services (The New York Times, National Public Radio, The Wall Street Journal, BBC News, etc.), blogs, and other commercial sites (Apple, ESPN, Orbitz, People, Salon, Yahoo!, eBay, etc.). Even the government has embraced RSS.

Without going into a lot of technical detail, RSS is an application of XML (eXtensible Markup Language), which is why you'll sometimes see the availability of feeds represented by XML. An item in an RSS feed usually contains a headline, an excerpt of the story, and a link to the full story.

GETTING STARTED

To take advantage of the convenience of RSS, you'll need a special piece of software (called a "newsreader" or "aggregator") to collect, organize, and display all your feeds.

the wider community can automatically receive updates when new information is added through daily, weekly and monthly RSS feeds.

Another important RSS-based service allows users to create feeds based on search terms within catalogues. These searches are automatically run when new records are added to the catalogue, and the feeds alert users to new content pertaining to their subjects of interest. An example of this is the University of Pittsburgh's PittCat+, a beta version of the catalogue which offers personalised, up-to-date book lists via RSS feeds. The feed is based on the regular running of a search string. Access to the catalogue and this service is also offered on the library's Facebook page.

Weblogs and micro-blogs

RSS can be used as a means of delivery for content created with other Web 2.0 tools. For instance, libraries with weblogs or blogs can provide

Figure 3.2 NorthStarNet aggregate calendar

regular automatic updates to users through RSS feeds. A blog in its most basic form is an online diary, where each entry is dated; entries are viewed from the most recent, with older entries often accessible in a yearly archive. Some of the popular blog services, such as Bloglines and Google Reader, not only provide for easy implementation but also for a range of functionality. If there are blogs which librarians think might be of interest to users, especially subject speciality blogs for reading, these also can be made available on the library website. As with RSS, blogs have been a favourite Web 2.0 tool among US and UK early-adopter libraries, again because there are many good free packages that can be offered directly on websites. Although many libraries use blogs for announcing events or posting messages from senior management (library director blogs seem to be popular in the USA), this tool also offers the opportunity of creating or tapping into a community of shared interests, whether by encouraging comment or including feeds, videos, podcasts and other sources on the page. While all blogs begin as one person talking to him or herself (although there are options for group blogs), the real Web 2.0 use is to have an exchange of ideas. There are many examples of libraries using blogs on their corporate websites, especially in the USA (UK examples are considered in the next chapter). Ann Arbor District Library in Michigan provides an example not just of blog implementation, but of its integration into the structure of the library's entire website. Through the use of Drupal, open source content management software (see later in this chapter), the library has attached blogging functionality to each page, with the result that users are able to address questions and comments as they browse pages (instead of having to find the 'contact us' page).

As with RSS feeds, blogs are productive for libraries when there is a particular target audience. In the best cases, the library becomes the conduit or the facilitator through which users can communicate. In Ann Arbor's case, the library found that without much prompting, the highest level of participation centred around the announcement of a gaming event (Figure 3.3), resulting in an increased level of discussion among users. According to Michelle McLean (2007), as of 2007 'their blogs have had 10,000 comments, but over 9,000 of those have been on the gaming blog'.

I am going to hazard a guess here and say that micro-blogging, and especially the hot website of the moment, Twitter, has become more popular with libraries than blogging ever was. Note I said 'libraries' and not 'librarians': individual librarians have taken to blogging in a big way. The evidence is fairly clear on sites that list webpages and services, such

Figure 3.3 Ann Arbor District Library events blog

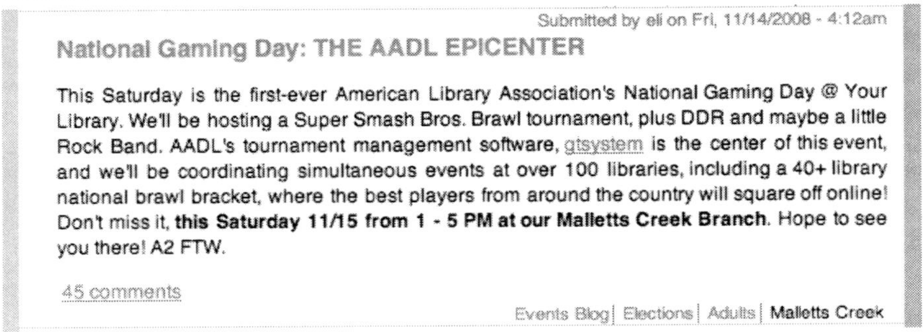

Submitted by eli on Fri, 11/14/2008 - 4:12am

National Gaming Day: THE AADL EPICENTER

This Saturday is the first-ever American Library Association's National Gaming Day @ Your Library. We'll be hosting a Super Smash Bros. Brawl tournament, plus DDR and maybe a little Rock Band. AADL's tournament management software, gtsystem is the center of this event, and we'll be coordinating simultaneous events at over 100 libraries, including a 40+ library national brawl bracket, where the best players from around the country will square off online! Don't miss it, **this Saturday 11/15 from 1 - 5 PM at our Malletts Creek Branch**. Hope to see you there! A2 FTW.

45 comments

Events Blog | Elections | Adults | **Malletts Creek**

as the Open Directory Project (DMOZ). Libraries, on the other hand, have given blogging a good try, but, as observed above, have generally not achieved much beyond one-way communication of events, and even these kind of pages seem to be a bit of a challenge for libraries to keep current.

However, in a matter of months libraries and librarians have taken to Twitter, if searches in Twellow, the Twitter Yellow Pages, or the Just Tweet It directory are anything to go by. It seems to be the rage across a diverse population of users, from presidents, the US Congress and the UK Parliament to the usual tech geeks, some of them library tech geeks. Of course, there have been the inevitable problems which may lead to a bit of backlash concerning its use by government representatives, as in the UK and USA alike there have been some prominent cases of inappropriate content. Whatever the problems, micro-blogging looks to be around for a while, and that seems all to do with the immediacy of the one-to-many contact as well as the ease of use. If a standard blog is an online diary, then a micro-blog looks like brief entries on a calendar. Like standard blogging, micro-blogging allows one person to talk directly to a number of people. However, content is delivered in brief messages (Twitter restricts to 140 words), which can be sent from mobile phones or PCs. Much the same as with blogging, updates can be delivered to users or 'followers' from a central site; however, although registration is required for those who want to send messages and those who want to receive them automatically (or 'follow') from specific accounts, no registration is required to view messages for a specific account on the Twitter website. This is a major and not insignificant difference between Twitter and other social networking services, such as

Facebook, where only those who have been accepted as 'friends' can read. Most mobile phones have Twitter software and, as with the Facebook application for mobiles, messages can be sent to the Twitter website and to followers on the go.

The best-publicised example of Twitter use here in the UK is Stephen Fry stuck in an elevator! At the time of writing, he is the third most popular Twitter user in the UK, although judging from teens like Matthew Robson as well as other research (see Chapter 1), it is exactly Fry and his generation who would seriously put young people off of Twitter. It would seem to be a mistake to create Twitter feeds in order to attract only teens. Even the founders of Twitter acknowledge that although it was originally conceived as a social tool, like Facebook and MySpace, a number of businesses, professionals, governments and activists alike have adapted it for their use because of its 'one-to-many' delivery. It is this 'one-to-many' combined with the immediacy functionality that has led the likes of Michael Arrington (2009) and Steve Gillmor (2009) at *TechCrunch* to predict the demise of the standard blog and RSS in favour of such popular 'real-time' services as Twitter and Facebook.

Regardless of the hype, there are, of course, the naysayers. According to Greenfield (2009) in a *Daily Mail* article:

> My fear is that these technologies [social technologies like Facebook, Twitter and Bebo] are infantilising the brain into the state of small children who are attracted by buzzing noises and bright lights, who have a small attention span for the moment.

While this is a sobering thought, there are uses for micro-blogging in public libraries which might not endanger children or adults (Figure 3.4). Twitter messages, or tweets, are not as onerous to generate as blog entries, as the emphasis is on brevity and real-time delivery, much like texts. The restriction on the length of messages is what makes micro-blogging a perfect fit for libraries looking to publicise events, new books or services. In addition, TwitPics provides a photo-sharing service, again to be delivered immediately to wherever followers happen to be. Twitter also offers an application, Twitter Grader, for rating profiles according to number of followers and the scope of the communication. This service provides libraries with the ability to assess their profiles not just among the Twitter community, but among the local community whose members may be following other local services on the site.

Figure 3.4 Scottish Libraries on Twitter

On the *Shifted Librarian* blog, Jenny Levine (2009) suggested a number of creative uses for Twitter, all essentially to promote libraries. Suggestions, modelled on those for museums, included 'funny things said by visitors; jokes, recipes, quotes, and interesting facts; institutional superstitions or weird things about the building; topical provocative questions; a daily or weekly feature on a specific topic'. As correctly observed in the comments to this blog entry, library Twitter feeds tend to repeat information that can be found elsewhere, such as event announcements, which do not invite much interaction and therefore reflect more traditional, Web 1.0 use. Adapting any one of these ideas would be entering more into the Web 2.0 spirit of the tool.

Some librarians are trying to implement Twitter as part of their virtual reference service. On the face of it, it is a quick way for users on the go to get help with questions. However, there are certain challenges to ease of use for the local public library community at large: users have to be registered on the site, and have to be a follower of the library in question in order for a transaction to occur. Moreover, there is no confidentiality: questions and answers will be public. A possible solution to some of these challenges is for the Twitter feed to somehow be linked into a library's instant messaging or other structured enquiry service; for example, OCLC is looking into a link between Twitter and its QuestionPoint product. Another solution suggested is to go after the users instead of waiting for them to follow the library: in other words, some librarians have adopted the approach of searching out or anticipating queries raised within the existing Twitter community at large or those from their own community registered and identifiable on the site, instead of waiting for their local users to register and find them.

In fact, Twitter seems to have an application for any type of use of the service: as of February 2009, Leena Rao at *TechCrunch* was able to list the top 21, based on a minimum number of visits, and I have seen more recent figures ranging from approximately 300 to 1,000. Twitter encourages users to create their own apps, so the 1,000 figure may even be low. For me, it is difficult to get a sense of the direction of the service from a business and longevity of popularity perspective. Is it truly revolutionary or a flash in the pan? Will it go the way of MySpace, taking with it library pages, hopes and dreams? A recent Harvard study suggests that the 'Twitterati' are still a relatively small group. According to Heil and Piskorski (2009):

> the top 10% of prolific Twitter users accounted for over 90% of tweets. On a typical online social network, the top 10% of users account for 30% of all production. To put Twitter in perspective, consider an unlikely analogue – Wikipedia. There, the top 15% of the most prolific editors account for 90% of Wikipedia's edits. In other words, the pattern of contributions on Twitter is more concentrated among the few top users than is the case on Wikipedia, even though Wikipedia is clearly not a communications tool. This implies that Twitter resembles more of a one-way, one-to-many publishing service more than a two-way, peer-to-peer communication network.

Of course, a comparison of Twitter and Wikipedia is that of a service in its infancy and a fully mature service. There is a chance that the 10 per cent may grow even within the next few months.

Podcasts

In this day and age, all things audio and visual are the dominant forms of delivering content on the web, so that blogging, for instance, need not be about communicating through the written word only but through other forms of media, such as audio and video podcasts (or vodcasts). Podcasts are essentially media files that can be downloaded over the internet using PCs, laptops, MP3 players and phones. There are numerous sites offering third-party podcasts which can be featured on library websites. Depending upon the target audience for information delivered in this way, librarians must be aware that not all users may have access to the appropriate software or have the requisite bandwidth. As observed above, it is, in its delivery, not interactive in any immediate sense, although discussion or text blog functionality can be attached for subsequent comment.

However, podcasts also pose an excellent opportunity for libraries to collaborate with members of the public to create and disseminate content. A number of libraries create their own podcasts featuring bibliographic instruction, library guides and interviews with authors and local politicians, quite a few of which can be found on Podcast Alley, a comprehensive directory of podcasts. One way of getting users involved and raising the library profile in the community is for libraries to podcast local events on their websites. For example, Multnomah County Library, through its Zine Library Group, ensures that non-traditional publications like self-published cartoons are not only represented in the library collection, but that local authors have a chance to raise their profiles through participation in such events as the Stumptown Comic Fest. The event also burnished the image of the library among young people in the city. Cathy Camper (2009) recorded the following feedback to the event and the library's involvement: 'I never thought my library would buy my comics, pay me to speak, catalog my work, and podcast my talk! Thank you so much!... Thanks for getting the library to sponsor us broke cartoonists!'

It pays to share: photos, video, music, social networking

RSS, blogs and podcasts are, regardless of how they are developed, primarily about communication one way: there is functionality to allow users to give feedback depending upon the software and the site, but even with blogs the motivation is imparting information about something, with little opportunity for users to augment or change that something. In its predominant manifestation, a blog is one person's diary, about the individual's thoughts, activities, ideas. The feedback, while desirable, is incidental.

To a certain extent, some of the same things can be said about sharing sites and services for photographs, videos and music. For the most part, what is uploaded to these sites is not subject to change by users. However, the emphasis is on sharing – no one person's contribution is paramount; all are available for comment. In addition, in their capacity as social networking services, their main objective is community and collaboration.

Of course, the use of different types of media in the library environment requires a bit more planning than a blog entry, and if it is aimed at users, all of the marketing advice such as knowing the target audience and building the motivation to participate pertains. Some of the library videos, for example, can be a bit stagey, a bit geeky (but in a good, entertaining way for the most part!). One of the best uses of a video connected to library services does not feature libraries or librarians, but kids talking about their favourite books, pretty much video book reports, on the StoryTubes website. StoryTubes is essentially a video book-report contest for children in the USA and Canada. Kids submit their videos, which can include a summary of the content, acting out scenes, dressing as characters or any other means of communicating their love for their favourite books. These videos can then be viewed on the site or on YouTube. The best are selected by online voting. Entry forms, release forms and publicity materials are provided by teachers and librarians who, with parents, help the kids put together their submissions. According to the site, schools and libraries work together as a team:

> Schools often secured parental permission, worked with students to develop their online booktalks, and provided technical expertise to tape and upload the entries. Public library partners structured the contests, provided the staff time to review entries and manage the event, and secured prizes.

This partnership, consisting of the libraries, schools and families, is not just an example of Web 2.0 collaborative content creation, but also of the combination of a new technology and approach to promote one of the traditional offerings of libraries, the love of reading and books. I especially love the chicken girl (Figure 3.5), and the comments on YouTube for her submission. It seems she had quite a few fans from Second Life communities, and her video has been added to the Mad City Chicken group on YouTube (I was afraid to look…).

YouTube is the video equivalent of photo sharing. StoryTubes is one such example of libraries, especially in the USA, raising the profile of services on the site, and it is one among many. Library videos range from library directors addressing their local communities (Allen Town Public Library) to promoting library services (Worthington Ohio Libraries' Just Read It!) to the truly wacky (see McCracken County Library's 'Super librarian'), although the Worthington video could be in this category as well! In fact, Worthington has a number of far-out videos, including one based on 'Thriller'. For those who don't know Weird Al, you have to look at his site – I can't do it justice here.

Librarians may get the impression that among the millions of videos on YouTube that include music, a library video of the same type would go relatively unnoticed, and at any rate be covered under some kind of

Figure 3.5   StoryTubes on YouTube

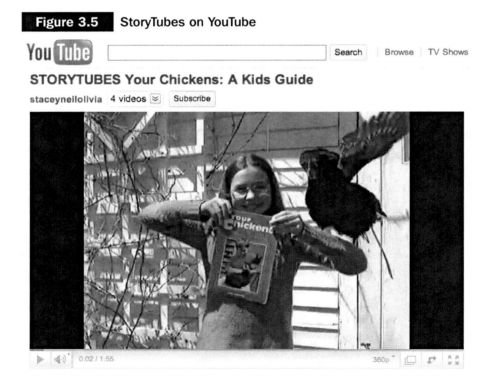

fair-use clause. Taking into account the amount of libraries that use music to accompany their videos – it's pretty much *de rigueur*, as watching people check out books or search stacks or computers cries out for a soundtrack at the very least – this last seems likely. However, a staff training video at Saint Joseph County Public Library ran afoul of Warner and to a certain extent YouTube itself when it used Madonna's song 'Ray of Light'. Michael Stephens (2009) was contacted by YouTube about use of the song, after he had made every effort to reach the appropriate people at Warner for permission. He admitted on his blog that the video may not have been covered under current copyright law as he had used the entire song and not selections of it. This, I think, left him believing he did not have a case to make with YouTube (and apparently there may or may not be dire consequences if they think their time has been wasted with spurious disputes: see Jessamyn West (2009)). He removed the music from the video. However, in the case of Warner clients there are indications that the corporate concerns are not just down to the fear of millions lost through library videos. Apparently, YouTube has had an ongoing feud with Warner that has resulted in the pulling of videos of Madonna and a number of artists from the site. According to Pete Cashmore (2009) at *Mashable*, the disagreement extended to the removal of songs from an artist's own website 'because the group used YouTube embeds. Meanwhile, YouTube users posted angry responses after seeing their videos muted or deleted.' Things seem to get a bit more ugly and even Orwellian where music on the web is concerned.

YouTube and other media-sharing web services provide a multifunctional platform for sharing content. For instance, Flickr is not only used for photo sharing and management, it also provides the opportunity for users to create blogs in which entries (and photos) feed into one aggregate blog. In this way, users can promote their own photos or highlight publicly available photos. Groups form around specific interests in Flickr, as in YouTube (those mad chickens!). In a sense, for libraries it is like social bookmarking sites in that, through the third-party environment and specifically away from their home environments, library services and librarians become part of the hive and are more open to sharing their content in an unrestricted way.

Because of this environment, Flickr has become popular with libraries, and I would hazard a guess to say more popular with UK public libraries than YouTube, with varying results. The best examples essentially create a 'photo branch library' environment, such as that provided by the Thomas Ford Memorial Library (Figure 3.6). The page consists of photos as descriptors for services and resources. So, for instance, photos are used to publicise events and activities, such as concerts and lectures at the library. In addition, the library uses the site to promote books, displaying photos of book jackets (Figure 3.7). There is a photo of its attractive library card as well – sort of library card as art *and* inducement to becoming a library member.

Arguably, all of this sharing of content began with peer-to-peer or social music service sites, like the ill-fated Napster (still with us in a somewhat altered state). The reason it is last in this grouping is quite honestly because I have had a difficult time finding library offerings of or participation in social music services (for an overview, perhaps somewhat dated, see Stewart (2007) which includes some of the stalwarts of Web 2.0 music, such as Pandora, last.fm and iLike). Library use of music-sharing sites is considerably behind that of photo sharing and even video sharing: this may be related to a fear of litigiousness (see YouTube example above), licensing restrictions or simply because corporate firewalls will not allow it. Whatever the reason, and it may be a combination of all three, the few examples I have found appear on library social networking pages, in other words far away from corporate pages. I mentioned Worthington Libraries above and its fun promotional videos, but it is also into music sharing through a MySpace page, Worthington Libraries Teens or Worthingteens (Figure 3.8). The library makes use of a MySpace 'pop-out' music player to feature songs chosen by teen librarians. The Worthingteens blog on the main library site automatically sends feeds to the MySpace page, as well as a Facebook

Figure 3.6 Thomas Ford Memorial Library on Flickr

Figure 3.7 Thomas Ford Memorial Library

page. Lancaster Library (UK) also uses the pop-out player for music as well as videos and podcast interviews with musicians on its MySpace 'Get it loud in libraries' page. The ExploreMusic library and site at Gateshead Libraries (UK) are notable for provision of music software, encouraging the creation as well as appreciation of music. As yet software delivery is provided purely in the library rather than online. However, users are encouraged to share their loops, scores and knowledge online for others to comment on, nurturing a supportive online environment. The 'free' music downloads offered on the site are samples from a subscription service to promote use. Users wanting to download music are directed out to various sites from a Music Links Directory page.

Quite a few libraries in the USA offer similar music download subscription services, most notably through Overdrive, a well-known and respected media services supplier (I have to confess that I

Figure 3.8 Worthingteens

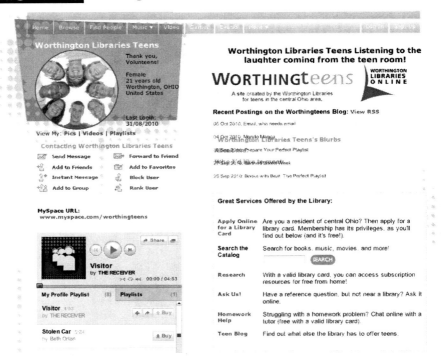

collaborated on an e-books project some years ago with Overdrive). The music offering that is part of its Digital Library Reserve Platform appears quite wide-ranging. As with most music (and e-books, which Overdrive provides as well) offerings to libraries, the content is available on one platform, in this case DRM-protected Windows Media Audio. According to the site, the music can be transferred to compatible devices or even burned to a CD, probably an option which only a very few publishers would allow.

Your space or mine? Social networking services

In much the same way as a Flickr page can and should be considered as a 'virtual branch' library page, a page on Facebook or MySpace can perform the same function by raising the library profile among non-users, whether they are from the immediate community or from the wider digital community. Social networking services are designed primarily for creating social groups, but increasingly public and private sector organisations, such as museums and libraries as well as businesses, are joining in. The groups evolve around specific interests, and the pages within the site offer the means by which new members can be accepted into the social group and communicate with individuals and across the group. Once registered, users can build personal pages that include media, such as photos, videos and podcasts, as well as blogs, Twitter, RSS feeds, Delicious and other social bookmarking tools. Other registered users who request it can have access to everything on an individual's page. MySpace is an exception in that it doesn't require registration to view pages.

Facebook and MySpace are relatively popular with libraries, with quite a few maintaining pages on both sites (although the popularity of MySpace has diminished to such a degree that the company had massive layoffs in June 2009). For the most part, the pages contain information about events and services, and a number of US libraries offer direct access to local catalogues and WorldCat. Facebook offers some reading applications and pages of potential use to librarians, such as Book weRead and Bookshare.

The best pages, however, make use of the kind of functionality that perhaps cannot be found or delivered on the main library page. In this sense, the pages are similar to webpages for branch libraries, of the kind with services not to be found on the library's corporate webpage. For example, the Lancaster and Worthington Libraries' MySpace pages both offer music applications that are not likely to be found on the corporate websites. That is not to say that they don't have some traditional offerings, like signing up for a library card, searching the catalogue and homework help, but these are not the primary focus of the pages. What is important is that they have built the pages around dedicated, web-savvy user groups, teenagers and music devotees. We will see in the section on the social catalogue as well as in the next chapter how crucial building this kind of participatory framework early in service development is.

I am still not entirely convinced that organisational pages belong on these sites, where the focus is on social groups, as opposed to sites that are communication tools like Twitter. Libraries in particular tend to put their pages together using content from the corportate site, including the inevitable events and activities announcements, and then promptly forget about them. I admit I didn't look at every single library page on Facebook and MySpace, but of those I trawled through, a majority had either a perfunctory or a desparate air about them. One of the most nonsensical announcements on a library Facebook page I have seen was for a book discussion group – to meet in the library. Why not take advantage of the digital environment, and have a virtual group meet and discuss on the social networking site? Wouldn't that be a great way to pull in those not within the local community or the existing core group of library users? It just confirms the perception that libraries are inclined to use Web 2.0 tools as bulletin boards.

Where the social group is not well targeted, unlike the very focused pages of Lancaster and Worthington, the lack of action on a page is offputting to say the least. Lack of updates and new content shows the library doesn't care, and the lack of feedback from users shows that they are not interested. And, in this context, it is difficult to understand what the significance of the count of 'friends' or 'champions' is: most seem low, in the hundreds if the library is lucky. But shouldn't a successful site have a much higher number for it to be worth the library's time? (In its social use, Facebook and MySpace users are notoriously interested in their popularity as indicated by their 'followers' and 'friends'.) Or are we to regard this designation for libraries as akin to 'friends of the library group'? For quite a few of the public library pages, this designation seems to include other library staff and authors whose books have been featured on the page or the corporate site. There is certainly not enough research on the traffic on library social networking sites to know what success looks like, and if it has been achieved by any library yet.

Stepping way outside the library! Virtual worlds

It is one thing to set up a Facebook page, where there is little direct interaction with users. It is quite another thing actually to staff a branch in a virtual world, an opportunity offered by Second Life and other virtual world sites. In these virtual worlds, avatars or 3D characters are created through which users interact with each other, in a similar way to video games. In Second Life users can set up a house, business and cultural organisations and institutions, such as libraries, universities and museums. Some libraries, and it does seem to be academic libraries mainly (perhaps because of the learning potential), have taken to Second Life in a big way.

A good look inside Second Life for the uninitiated is provided, of course, through another social networking site, YouTube. There are a number of tutorials which help with creating an account and using the software – see, for example, Peakdavid (2008) 'Second Life tutorial: beginner guide – create account & get started in Second Life', created for University of Maryland students. Although a foreigner to SL myself, one cannot help but note that there seems to be a significant library presence on the site. This impression is not solely derived from the citations of presentations given within SL (see Lankes et al., 2007), but from reports of non-librarians. For example, 'Rik Reil' (Rikomatic, 2006) has provided a tour of Info Island on YouTube, and in his blog describes its launch:

> I got an invite to the official opening of the Info Island Second Life Library, a project I have been watching develop for the past six months with great interest. Those librarians have a whole weekend full of activities planned from October 12–14, from panel discussions to scary movies, a costume ball, a beach party, to a bioterrorism demonstration! You can see the complete invitation and program after the jump. If you haven't been in awhile, Info Island has really blossomed into an incredible campus of libraries and information resources about both the virtual world and the real one. I got so excited, I created a little video of me touring the island. Not only is it a great place to visit, it's a cool place to practice your skating. Thanks to Torley Linden, for awesome 'free as in beer' music. (This is a higher res version you can download.)

Info Island began as the virtual presence of the Alliance Library System Illinois on Second Life (Figure 3.9). The services offered by the library grew (it is now known as the Community Virtual Library), and as Alliance formed partnerships with other organisations, so did Info Island. Judging from the extensive programme of activities over a number of days of the grand opening, the launch and services represented a large-scale international collaboration. Activities involved everything from the opening of subject-specific libraries to costume balls and beach parties (for a detailed schedule of events and participants, see Alliance Library System, 2006).

However, although it is a virtual world, services, programmes and even buildings and staff do not come cheaply. At one point there were plans to build Renaissance Island, an educational tool to replicate the environment of Elizabethan England. According to a project summary on *NetSquared* (Bell, 2007), to build a Second Life version of Greenwich Castle would cost $2,000! Interestingly, a response to this project

Figure 3.9 A view of Community Virtual Library on Second Life

proposal from Ivan Boothe (2007) echoes some of the concerns I have about libraries and social networking: 'But, take away the technology for your proposal, and this seems to just be a public education campaign. We could just as easily be funding a flyering campaign about the Renaissance. Second Life *is* cool, but the presence of the campaign in SL alone doesn't create social networking.'

Part of the social networking would be taking advantage of the technology to co-create library services – library users and librarians putting together a Renaissance Island. I know that Alliance works with other types of organisations, but it is not clear what participation is from those who would actually use the service. Indeed, I have not been able to confirm how many library environments in Second Life have been 'co-developed' or is this a case of traditional library environments duplicated in a virtual world? Of course, SL is filled with straightforward replication of the 'real world', apparently right down to the Linden dollars and cents, and it may be unfair to hold libraries to a standard not universally adopted within the site. There have been reports that users are drifting away from the site as the whole environment begins to replicate physical reality, something that a massively multiplayer online role-playing game (MMORPG), like War of the Worlds, definitely avoids. (For more on number of users on SL see Shirky (2007).)

Most of the applications of gaming in libraries involve hosting gaming clubs and websites, and publishing gaming news. Although there is no indication that libraries will develop games or that these virtual worlds will somehow be integrated into library systems, supporting these clubs provides a perfect opportunity to raise the profile of libraries among the universally hard-to-reach groups, especially pre-teen and teenage boys. As Ann Arbor found, this new demographic group are ripe for using the social networking tools on library sites, and are indeed savvy web users who could make a significant contribution to social catalogues in their specific subject interest. Indeed, public libraries are increasingly turning to incorporating gaming into services. A summary of a study conducted with US public libraries by the American Library Association (2009a) reports that:

> Four hundred randomly selected public libraries responded to the survey. The study found that at least seven out of every 10 supported gaming, four out of 10 public libraries run gaming programs, including both board and Web-based games, and more than eight out of 10 libraries allowed patrons to play games on library computers.

Nicholson (2007) wrote, 'Over the last few years, some libraries have been turning to gaming activities like Dance Dance Revolution as a way of bringing in new demographic groups and exposing them to library services.'

Such is the appreciation for what can be gained by gaming, especially in the area of literacy, that the American Library Association (2009b), with a $1 million grant from the Verizon Foundation, has developed an online toolkit, the 'Librarian's guide to gaming'.

Putting it all together: start pages and mash-ups

For libraries struggling with corporate IT strictures on Web 2.0 use, start pages may offer the solution. Access to a number of the resources mentioned above, as well as those following, can be gathered together on a single site, hosted by third-party companies offering customisable software. I have seen these start pages referred to as a 'home away from home', because as web-based tools they can be created and maintained on home PCs as well as accessed and modified from anywhere. For public libraries within a controlled web environment they afford more freedom from corporate security, branding and design. They can be personalised according to library, instead of corporate, services and objectives and provide for more interactivity and experimentation. If a library is having difficulty with incorporating Web 2.0 tools on its corporate site, a start page may provide a more productive outlet. Some of the better-known services are Pageflakes, Netvibes and iGoogle. An interesting use of this Web 2.0 tool in a library setting can be found on the Nashville Public Library website, where each branch library has its own start page.

For libraries with a bit more resident expertise, quite a few of these tools can be combined to create another entirely unique website or service. This combination of tools and content is known as a mash-up. The current favourite basis for the mash-up among librarians is Google Maps and photos from a Flickr account (which usually also includes an RSS feed). I have seen statements that mash-ups are easy to produce, but I am not sure that the average librarian would not be daunted by the prospect, and for UK public libraries, technical restrictions would make them difficult to produce on a corporate site. However, there is mash-up editor software that assists in the creation and editing of content, such as Google Mashup Editor. James Smith at Sunderland Libraries in the UK has created just such a mash-up to focus on a specific aspect of the area's history: bomb damage during the Second World War (Figure 3.10).

Somewhere in the middle: wikis

The tools mentioned thus far are either designed for one-to-many communication or else can be used as such, and quite often are by librarians. If it is not the librarian's intention to interact, then the fact that blogs and social networking services go without feedback is of little concern, until, of course, someone usually in senior management wonders what benefit is derived. There are other Web 2.0 tools that demand interaction, and without user feedback or participation their implementation would definitely be considered a failure. These tools do require more work and commitment on the part of library staff, and actually move users and librarians closer to the co-created library. We will look at such tools as folksonomies and social catalogues, but first I'd like to consider a tool that falls between the two categories, the wiki.

Figure 3.10   Sunderland Libraries mash-up: 'Their past, your future'

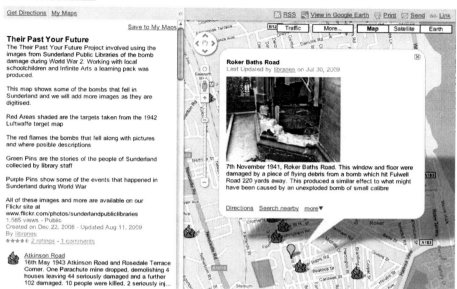

Library-sponsored wikis allow for users to collaborate directly in, for the most part, an open environment to produce and share documents, whether for creative or business purposes. A wiki is one or a group of webpages enabled for global modification, something like a Word document that everyone can modify or add to, and which carries a record of those changes. While the concept is for global participation, 'global' usually refers to those who have registered or have been allowed into the community. Of course, this makes eminent sense from the perspective of quality assurance and security, especially for small-scale wikis with a very narrow focus and target audience. However, it is interesting to note that even Wikipedia, the best known of all wikis, provides the following message when an editing hopeful clicks on the 'edit this page' tab:

> You are not currently logged in. Editing this way will cause your IP address to be recorded publicly in this page's edit history. If you create an account, you can conceal your IP address and be provided with many other benefits. Messages sent to your IP can be viewed on your talk page.

Which, of course, provides the inducement for most users, in the interests of privacy, to create an account.

In libraries, though, wikis do not necessarily have the free-for-all atmosphere that the Wikipedia environment indicates. In fact, quite a few are used for staff or as part of training. Matthew Bejune (2007) estimated that of the libraries studied, almost 75 per cent used wikis for collaboration across libraries or among staff. Of the wikis that were dedicated to public use, most constituted the creation of content, such as bookmarks, *for* users by librarians. One such examples is GRPLpedia, developed by Grand Rapids Public Library Michigan and described on the site as a 'fanatastic encyclopedia of WikiGuides or subject guides put together by librarians'. 'Library success: a best practices wiki', developed by Meredith Farkas with the contributions of librarians, identifies a number of library wikis which seem to be predominantly created and updated by librarians. Some libraries, mostly university libraries, offer students and faculty the opportunity to comment on bibliographic and reference content.

So far, so much the same as the above Web 2.0 tools: one-way communication, no real building of a community. However, in keeping with their original purpose, wikis can be used to co-create libraries, to foster participation between libraries and users to a degree that is not necessarily possible with the other Web 2.0 tools mentioned above. A wiki is not really a communication tool so much as a creative tool, and yes, one person can use it to create, but then why use a wiki? Its very nature demands collaboration over the web, and when librarians use it for its dedicated purpose, they are truly on their way to building community, building participation. In this way, wikis are a kind of bridge between the first set of tools and those considered below.

There are some brave public librarians sharing wikis with their community. Princeton Public Library experimented with a 'book-lovers wiki' in 2006/2007, as part of a summer reading programme. Those who wanted to contribute e-mailed the library first and were subsequently sent instructions for uploading a review and a password for access. As with BiblioCommons below, users were offered prizes for participation. One of the more promising wiki implementations, the Book Case, will be reviewed in a case study in the next chapter.

Do librarians really trust the wisdom of the crowd? Folksonomies, social bookmarking, tagging, social catalogues

I suppose if I had to vote for the Web 2.0 tool that would most fill librarians with fear and loathing it would have to be folksonomies (known also as social classification, social or collaborative tagging, etc.). Because, in their truest Web 2.0/Library 2.0 implementation, they strike closest to the libraries' sense of professionalism, expertise and mission. I am sure, when it comes to user-created content in catalogues, some librarians would concur with Andrew Keen (2007) in *The Cult of the Amateur*: 'It's ignorance meets egotism meets bad taste meets mob rule on steroids.' Or 'It's alright on LibraryThing, but not on my catalogue you don't!' And, precisely because of these sentiments, I have to include wikis, used as intended, with this group of tools. All manner of scholarly types, from professors to librarians, and some not so scholarly have taken shots at the epitome of wikis, Wikipedia, precisely because of the apparent ungovernability of the hive mind in areas best left to the professionals. This attitude pervades the level of use of all these tools by librarians.

A way of defining a folksonomy is to contrast it with a taxonomy: essentially, a folksonomy is a method or system of devising descriptors or keywords (tags) online by users of any given resource, whereas a taxonomy is all that but developed by professionals, namely librarians. The perceived difference comes down to expertise. It is not the case that librarians generally disapprove of folksonomies: they are a good thing, democratic even when developed for LibraryThing or Flickr. But feelings run high when it comes to using this method for creating or even augmenting descriptors to be attached to a library catalogue record. This is library turf, as it were, and it goes to the very heart of the problem libraries have with Web 2.0 when it truly means user-generated content on their websites.

The manner in which librarians use folksonomies depends on how much input they are ready to allow their users. Folksonomies grow up around the activity of social bookmarking, which is basically the online organisation and management of internet bookmarks. Two popular tools, Delicious and Furl (which has now become part of Diigo), provide a space for users to save and organise bookmarks as well as create keywords, or tags, as finding tools. Individual bookmarks can be shared with others on the sites or through RSS feeds. Users can even bookmark library webpages or book records to be included with their own bookmarks on the sites. On the Nashville Public Library Teen Web page, teenage volunteers use Delicious to record and organise their bookmarks and then reference the Delicious tags on the page so that other users can access these resources (Figures 3.11 and 3.12).

A library's use of social bookmarking sites in this way creates an environment whereby users can learn from librarians not just about sites of special interest through the bookmarks themselves, but how to use Web 2.0 tools to create their own bookmarks. The teenage volunteers, with the help of librarians, accomplish this last by explaining where the bookmarks have been gathered and providing a link to the Delicious page giving information about the service. The library's use of the Delicious site helps to raise its profile with its own users, as it shows them that the library is open to using new and popular tools. In addition, the library increases its visibility among a wider audience: users on these sites and outside its immediate community could consider library bookmarks authoritative on any given subject area. By placing its resources and expertise in a community environment not necessarily

Figure 3.11   Nashville Public Library Teen Web

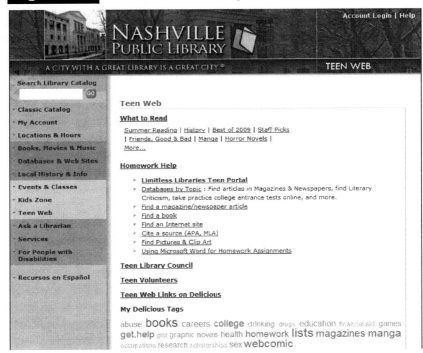

Figure 3.12 Nashville Public Library Delicious page

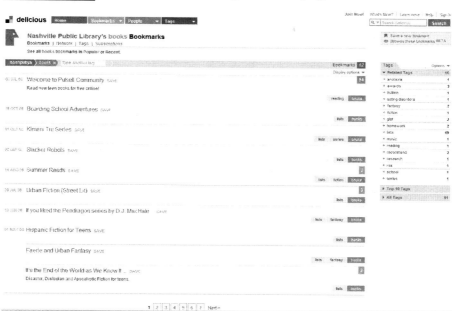

defined by geographic constructs, the library not only raises its own profile but that of public libraries in general.

Of course, the method of classification, the folksonomy, on these sites is created by the users. The most direct, seamless way to integrate social bookmarking and the creation of tags by users with library services is through the catalogue. This translates to users either contributing bookmarks or tagging library book records with keywords predominantly of their own devising or with the tags provided by the library. A creative variation on user-generated bookmarks is Ann Arbor's Card Catalog Images, which provides users with digitised catalogue cards upon which they can write notes, either for their own use or for the library's (Figure 3.13). These images are incorporated into user profiles.

An early manifestation of what are now commonly known as social catalogues was developed at Ann Arbor by John Blyberg, who then went on to Darien, Connecticut, where he has developed SOPAC (Social Online Public Access Catalog; see Figure 3.14). Both US libraries, as well as a few others, have taken up the real challenge for librarians when it comes to Web 2.0 implementation: letting users loose on the catalogue.

The social or sharing catalogue

As noted in Chapter 1, I bear the scars of trying to break down the silo that is the library online catalogue. There is much dissatisfaction over the inflexible nature of the predominantly proprietary systems found in most public libraries. Some librarians feel that, aside from the commercial constraints, there are other prohibitive aspects of the catalogue, such as the tyranny of the MARC record: it is too long, too complex, it contains information extraneous to users' needs. This concern has been addressed by some libraries and library management suppliers by shorter public catalogue records. However, R. David Lankes and colleagues (2007) maintain that instead of becoming more accessible, library catalogues are becoming less useful. In his Second Life presentation, Lankes compares the MARC/library catalogue record to the Amazon record, which is considerably longer. The difference is that the Amazon record is composed mainly of user-generated content – reviews, ratings, referrals. Although librarians may refer wistfully to Amazon, it still remains to be seen how many would want to adopt the degree of openness that would result in the user-generated catalogue record.

Amazon has essentially set the bar for how users expect to access databases, and especially book, video, CD and DVD databases, which are the primary stuff of library catalogues. One solution for libraries has been to offer the option to buy books from Amazon via the library

Figure 3.13 Ann Arbor Card Catalog Images

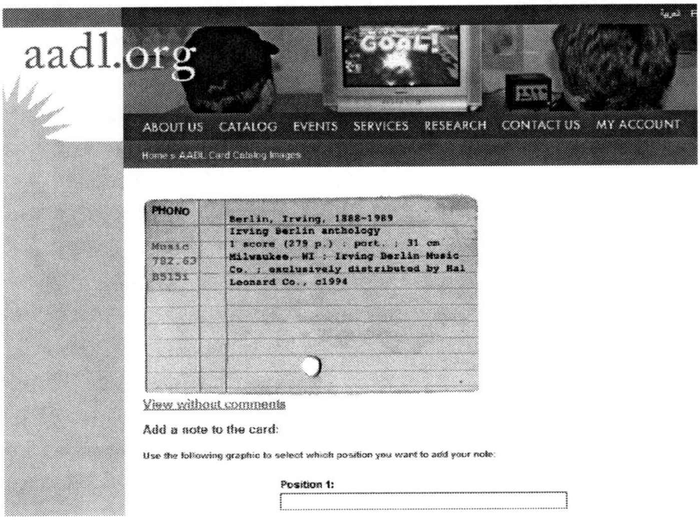

Figure 3.14 Darien Public Library's SOPAC

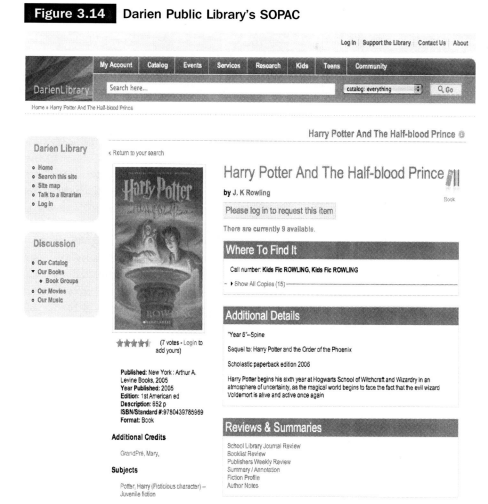

catalogues. The aim, though, should not be to drive users from the library site, from the inflexibility of the library catalogue to a much sleeker, more responsive model. Web 2.0 tools offer a more direct way of opening up the library catalogue to users. Kathy Gould of the Palos Verdes District Library in California, in recounting a conversation with Beth Jefferson from BiblioCommons, notes that 80–90 per cent of traffic on library websites goes to library catalogues, 'so it is a prime platform for social interaction' (Palos Verdes District Library, 2007). Jefferson (2009) is part of a development team responsible for an innovative example of a social catalogue, although she resists that phrase and maintains that BiblioCommons is an integrated library system (ILS), however unlike any other it is. Whatever they are called, software systems like BiblioCommons and SOPAC break down the silos of data.

Social catalogues are those online library systems which offer users the opportunity to provide feedback on books, videos, DVDs and anything subject to classification by a library, which is directly added to catalogue records. This feedback, in the form of a tag, review, recommendation or rating, can in turn be viewed by other users who may well respond with their own feedback. In this way, users are augmenting the catalogue record as well as the public-facing information provided for the material. As noted above, Beth Jefferson doesn't hold with the term; her contention is that the basic management system combined with the social software adds up to a new kind of ILS, but an ILS all the same. However, the opposite can obtain as well: the ILS with all the social enhancements of the tools reviewed here thus far resembles nothing so much as a social networking service, albeit one tied to a locality and local systems. Below we will see how LibraryThing, for example, is being used to enhance catalogue participation. But I can't help but ask myself when looking at these examples of social catalogues: is LibraryThing just improving catalogues, or are catalogues coming to resemble more and more social networking services like LibraryThing?

The first of the two most notable examples of social catalogues, the Darien Connecticut Public Library SOPAC, was launched in 2007. Darien's open source, locally hosted catalogue actually began life at Ann Arbor as SOPAC 1.0, and Blyberg (2008) is the first to admit that it would definitely not work 'out of the box' as it was customised to increase the functionality of the Ann Arbor catalogue. The software that is the foundation for SOPAC 2.0, developed for Darien Library, is the same as for 1.0; however, the objective was to build a product that could be used with any library management system. The original software, Drupal, works with two other software components to give users the option to create their own tags, provide ratings and write comments and reviews.

BiblioCommons, with funding and subscriptions from various Canadian library and cultural consortia, launched a live, proof-of-concept 'Social Discovery System' in 2008 at Oakville Public Library in Toronto (Figure 3.15). The key difference from SOPAC, from a technological and strategic perspective, is that BiblioCommons is centrally located to accommodate from the beginning a national user base and diverse library management systems. According to Norman Oder (2008), the population base represented by the current subscribers

Figure 3.15 Catalogue record from Oakville Public Library

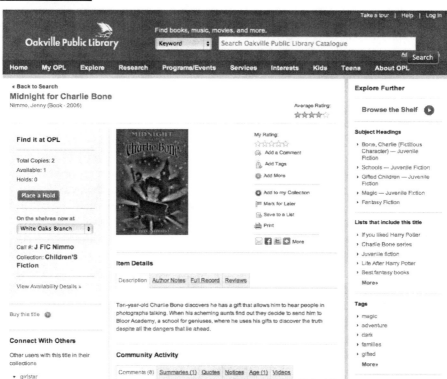

and funders constitutes 20 million of the national total of 33.2 million. As with SOPAC 2.0, the company has been doing its technical homework with a number of proprietary library system suppliers and enhancing, if not outright replacing, the user functionality of these systems.

However, a key objective for BiblioCommons is related to those population statistics: the building of the 'architecture for participation' or its participation framework. According to O'Reilly (2004), this concept refers to the 'nature of systems that are designed for user contribution'. Indeed, as O'Reilly points out, any site or service built with software or systems designed for communication is by definition participatory. In this sense, both BiblioCommons and SOPAC are based on participation architecture, as both systems facilitate participation in the creation of the catalogue. However, BiblioCommons has strategically moved beyond architecture to building a framework that combines a user participation base and motivation with the architecture right from beta phase.

Where Blyberg seems to be growing his system from 'one to many', in the sense that it is locally based but with application across systems, Jefferson has been working from a 'many to one' perspective, in that BiblioCommons is trying to grow a national user base from the centre at the same time that it is developing the product.

But the challenge still remains for both systems: how to build that critical mass of participation and get librarians to accept this new way of working with users to co-create the catalogue. Experimenting with RSS or Twitter is one thing – if a library cannot make a success of implementing one of these services, not a lot of time and money has been lost. What is immediately obvious and writ large with a catalogue, the very basis of online library business, is that implementing Web 2.0 software does not in and of itself guarantee use. With a catalogue, the silence can be deafening when users are not taking advantage of the functionality, as well as risky not just in a monetary sense but also in terms of the capacity used for development and promotion. The lack of reviews, user-generated tags and other types of participation is also obvious to regular catalogue users, who might be a bit disdainful of the library trying to be 'cool'. Beth Jefferson (2007), in one of the numerous talks she has given on BiblioCommons as a project and live service, remarked on the disparity of user reviews of *The Da Vinci Code* in OCLC's WorldCat and LibraryThing – at the time of the talk, two versus 400. Both services are built around a participation framework, based on that important combination of technology and critical mass of user motivation to contribute. The key difference is that while LibraryThing has targeted the wider web community from the beginning, essentially a 'born-Web 2.0' service, OCLC began life as a peer-to-peer desktop service. The company has only recently embarked on public-facing functionality through WorldCat. Still, it is clear that OCLC has some way to go change not only the general web user's perception, but also that of the usual library user, not necessarily familiar with the WorldCat offering.

An outcome of BiblioCommons thinking on the subject of participation is some of the marketing approaches employed in Oakville. One such is a prize incentive, including an iMac, a $100 gift certificate for books and arguably the most valuable of all, a visit to any public library in Canada, for two, of course (Figure 3.16). In order for users to be eligible for the prize draw, they have to earn 'community points' by commenting, tagging, summarising, providing referrals to similar titles

Figure 3.16 Promotion for contributing to Oakville catalogue

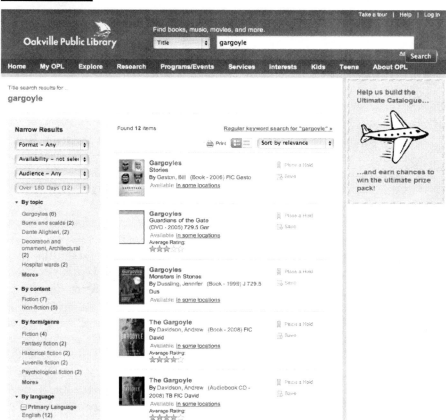

and indicating age suitability. Each of these activities earns a community credit.

A number of suppliers of proprietary library management systems, such as Talis and Axiell, are offering Web 2.0-enabled interfaces that can be integrated with catalogues. However, despite all this development, and despite the fact that contests and prizes may increase participation initially, the inherent problem has yet to be resolved: what's in it for users to tag records over a longer period? Participation in LibraryThing, Delicious and other social classification sites is driven by the users' requirement for a means to organise their own work and resources – in other words, from their personal interests or for purposeful use. This view gives rise to the question posed by Jonathan Rochkind (2008) from Johns Hopkins University:

So what personal benefit can a user get in tagging in a library catalog? If we provided better 'saved records' features, perhaps, keep tracks of books you've checked out, books you might want to check out, etc. But I'm not sure if our users actually *use* our catalogs enough to find this useful, no matter how good a 'saved records' feature we provide. In an academic setting, items from the catalog no longer neccesarily make up a majority of a user's research space.

However, user feedback in Oakville indicates that some feel there is more value to adding a review on a library site than on a commercial site (perhaps there is more of a sense of contributing to the local community?).[2] There is the expectation, and hope, that other activities on library sites may drive users to contribute to the catalogue. For instance, while actual responses to Ann Arbor's blog entries have not been numerous, there does appear to be a correlation between some of these entries and a rise in tagging of book records on related subjects. In addition, entries for new books quite often result in requests for these items through the catalogue. So, while there is no direct response to blogs, there is a response in the form of activities they prompt.[3]

At the moment, the lack of contribution on the part of the users may not even be the initial or primary concern for a good many librarians: it is the quality assurance, the application of library expertise that will be required when users do contribute. A way around this might be monitoring, but Jefferson disagrees with this approach on capacity (where are the staff and budget to do this?) and legal grounds (could the library be liable for editing that appears discriminatory?). Moreover, neither Blyberg nor Jefferson in their work with social catalogues has experienced the problem with which librarians are most concerned: inappropriate use. Neither system currently has any functionality for responding to this problem (see Jefferson (2009) podcast on social catalogues for a discussion on the systems with Blyberg and Jefferson). There are, however, some basic rules that can be applied, such as an authentication requirement and a user name that corresponds to a library account. These measures allow for some control in the event of unacceptable content.

Rochkind (2008) suggests that a way of maintaining control over the quality of tagging is not only for libraries to supply a set from which to choose, but also for this set to be supplied for all libraries to import from such centralised services as OCLC. OCLC, through WorldCat, could aggregate tags and supply a standardised set for libraries to use, in much the same way that libraries import standardised records including classification and keywords into local catalogues, and be used to receive standardised sets of catalogue cards. Rochkind describes such a service as 'low hanging fruit (a tagging interface on worldcat.org with a good API is not rocket science)'.

While OCLC has yet to go after the low-hanging fruit, LibraryThing has certainly seized the opportunity to widen its participation framework by developing a software platform that allows libraries to import Web 2.0 features, including its extensive tagging, into local catalogues. A fee-based service, LibraryThing for Libraries works with most library management systems through a catalogue overlay that increases the functionality of the public-facing features, providing much the same options for participation as SOPAC and BiblioCommons. One of the first libraries to implement the service, Claremont University Library in the USA (Westcott et al., 2009), has reported that it is relatively easy to implement and LibraryThing provides a good level of support (for more information on this and other tools which can be integrated with library management systems, see *Library Hi-Tech*, 27(1) special issue on next-generation OPACs). LibraryThing can also be used in conjunction with other OPAC enhancement tools like AquaBrowser. AquaBrowser is essentially a discovery tool which works with various library management systems as a catalogue overlay to enhance searching. Its own functionality has been increased through the development of MyDiscoveries, which adds the same type of user participation functionality standard for the social catalogue. It works with LibraryThing in that local user contribution through AquaBrowser combines with the contribution already resident in LibraryThing to create an even greater participation framework.

Conclusion

In this chapter, as we have ranged over a number of tools and good practice examples, there have been some pretty consistent recurring themes for those libraries truly interested in social networking: be clear on library objectives, understand user motivation, build the participation framework and select the technology tools appropriate to librarians and users alike. While quite a few of these tools can be used in the Web 1.0, one-to-many spirit, it is clear that libraries like Oakville, Darien and Ann

Arbor are after making their libraries and partnerships more visible on the web across a broader range of users. This is indeed development by revolution, although it remains to be seen whether the impact among users will have the desired effect.

There are some excellent examples here, good models to follow and follow up. But one could come away from the chapter thinking 'every library is doing something except for mine'. However, before giving in to the pressure or the enthusiasm generated by these examples without clearly articulating objectives, consider the experience of British libraries in the next chapter. At the national level, they are a case study of the incremental and revolutionary approach to online public library development. On an individual, case-by-case basis, they exemplify some of the issues identified in this chapter as well as some of the resolutions of those issues. We will see how, over the past 15 years, British libraries have accepted the challenge of social networking, some by jumping in with totally new services and others getting to Web 2.0 by increments.

Notes

1. However, I have become increasingly aware of this refrain as an excuse for the lack of evaluation of use of these services, termed by Booth (2007) as an 'evaluation bypass'. I am inclined to have some sympathy with this view of the lack of evaluation, especially given how long some libraries have been deploying these services.
2. Personal e-mail from Gail Richardson, manager, online services, Oakville Public Library, 5 May 2010.
3. Personal e-mail from Eli Neiburger, associate director for IT and production, Ann Arbor District Library, 29 April 2010.

Part III
By increment *and* revolution:
libraries getting to Web 2.0

4

A tale of one country

> Lots of activities that predate Web 2.0 created the fertile ground for applications based on radical trust to thrive. Some of these old technologies: telnet, gopher, and much of the first generation web were based on the culture of gifting – giving away information for free and seeing all kinds of positive things happen. There was a sense of wonder at all of this gifting of 'free information', especially at first, before we started to take it for granted. This tilled the soil and seeded the ideas that bloomed into the systems that combine 'radical trust' with 'participation'. (Fichter, 2006)

After that brisk romp through the highs of library Web 2.0 implementation, it would be understandable if some librarians are left feeling not only a bit behind in developing Web 2.0 services, but in general not prepared or supported for anything beyond experimentation, if that. The Web 2.0 champions (and also those who think Web 2.0 is so passé) either really don't know or care to acknowledge that there are quite a few libraries whose corporate sites are barely in advance of flat HTML pages. This is as true for UK libraries, where the websites are incorporated into and controlled by the larger local government digital environment, as it is for US libraries, where websites are not necessarily controlled or supported by local governments (although this can vary from state to state). This environment allows US libraries a degree of autonomy in website development and services, as well as design and branding, but also means that less well-resourced libraries have minimal web presences because quite simply they cannot afford to spend the money.

So, let's stop a bit, and in the best business case practice, assess where we are. I think the most productive way to do this is to step back and see where we have been and how we got there. There is plenty libraries are doing right now that is not Web 2.0 in the technology sense, but that is either in the spirit of social networking or at least provides the foundation or that participation framework upon which such services can be built. Accordingly, it is helpful to assess library services against the O'Reilly and Leadbeater hierarchies to understand what material librarians have to work with.

The challenge to libraries

I know that O'Reilly's (2006) and Leadbeater's (undated) hierarchies[1] may sound fairly rigorous in application to librarians, especially those just starting out with Web 2.0. It is true that they, as well as Darlene Fichter (2006), all challenge libraries globally to effect a shift in their common identity on the web, from information providers to service co-developers, thus becoming more visible to those outside their local communities. This challenge, combined with the perceived pressure that every library is doing something, might cause librarians to think that they have to go immediately into revolutionary mode.

It is true that O'Reilly's and Leadbeater's hierarchies are targeted more at the wider and especially the commercial world beyond library walls, and therefore prove more of a challenge to public-funded and often cash-strapped institutions. There is also a sense that websites at the highest levels of these hierarchies are to a certain extent Web 2.0-based commercial competition for library services (whether public institutions should or can compete with commercial organisations is another book). These hierarchies are to a certain extent representative of the current hype around Web 2.0 and communicate a certain inevitability and urgency to library online development in the medium to long term, especially as print continues to lose ground to digital.

However, while O'Reilly and Leadbeater are quite clear about what constitutes Web 2.0 implementation, for those libraries not always able to be on the upward curve of innovation as early adopters (see reference to diffusion of innovations in the Prologue), the hierarchies can be viewed from another perspective (granted not quite the purpose for which they were intended): that Web 2.0 implementation is not necessarily an either/or proposition, not at least for initial implementation or in the short term, but offers the opportunity to explore the new technology at a rate commensurate with capacity while taking in the larger implications of social networking. And to a certain extent, the various levels outlined in the hierarchies map on to the evolution of public libraries on the web. In turn, this evolution beginning as recently in the past as it did provides lessons as libraries move into the truly transformational territory of social networking. Fichter herself, as quoted above, notes that some of the 'old technologies' have provided the foundation for the transformation of web culture which has been ushered in by Web 2.0.

In the comments section to the O'Reilly (2006) article, a poster adapted O'Reilly's hierarchy of Web 2.0 applications to the history of publishing. Along the same lines, the review of the online evolution of public libraries in this chapter is approached using the levels of the hierarchy to understand better libraries' progress – and opportunities – online. Accordingly, we will move from implementation predating Web 2.0 up to some of the more daring examples of libraries developing Web 2.0-based services, all the while looking at specific examples and case studies from British libraries where, in the words of Fichter (2006), 'the soil has been tilled and seeds have been planted to create the systems combining radical trust and participation'. Reviewing British libraries' evolution online demonstrates where and how practically to make a start without having to think about changing the world, not just yet anyway.

Why British public libraries?

In September 2009 the British Society of Chief Librarians announced the launch of a multinational universal library card: a library card from just one locality, say Cambridgeshire, would unlock the collections of more than 4,000 libraries in England, Wales and Northern Ireland. Whether this constitutes a revolutionary leap for public libraries remains to be seen (for example, they haven't solved the electronic subscription question, nor the delivery aspect; users still have to return books to the library from which they were borrowed). But the initiative and others like it in the UK bring together some of the ideas and issues explored in previous chapters:

- the critical mass required for a participation framework upon which to launch large-scale services, social networking and otherwise

- incremental versus revolutionary progress, and which creates real change

- the requirement for sharply focused objectives regardless of whether a library is experimenting or creating real-time services demanded by this new technology.

Indeed, the almost 15 years since UK public libraries made their first forays on to the web are illustrative of not only the rapid progress libraries have made in the digital environment in general, but also the varying degree to which they participate over the physical network and are visible in the social network.

A bit of UK public library pre-history

The effort for any library to get on to the web in the first place was considerable, especially if, as in the case of British libraries, it was attempted much in advance of any comparable government service and without any support. In previous chapters I have made the distinction between Web 1.0 and Web 2.0. Web 1.0 for British libraries in the late 1990s was about getting content, which mainly consisted of information about services, opening times and location, on to an accessible webpage. As recently as 1996, few British public libraries had webpages. It was through EARL, the UK national public library networking consortium, that libraries for the first time were able to put information about their services on the web.

This content was not put on to local government servers, because few local governments themselves had websites or any kind of networked technical infrastructure (indeed, while researching this book, I found that Gateshead Libraries had initially maintained the local government's website):[2] the consortium had a dedicated server, where information about library services was uploaded and stored (libraries provided their details by sending either floppy disks or printed text through the mail), and provided access through the library portal, EARLWeb. This was a major step for public libraries: just getting basic information, like opening times and services, on to the web. Moreover, they also provided the data for web-based cooperative services like Familia (local history holdings), Magnet (journal and magazine holdings), Euroguide (European resources) and SignPost (foreign language collections). It was more than an incremental improvement; it was a radical, large-scale move into a totally new, unknown environment.[3]

This fairly revolutionary change was soon followed by another that would really propel all libraries in Britain into the digital environment, the People's Network. The impetus for the network was a 1997 report, 'The new library: the People's Network' (Matthew Evans Working Group, 1997). As a result, the government authorised funding of the project. From 2000 to 2003 over 30,000 PCs with broadband internet access and software applications were installed in over 4,000 libraries. The British government financed this massive undertaking, implemented by local library authorities, through three separate funding streams: £100 million for IT equipment and internet connections; £20 million for staff training; and £50 million for a digitisation programme. This massive initiative at once enabled libraries on a national scale to provide web use to the public and IT training for staff, not just for their own professional development but also so that they could support and facilitate public use. It laid the foundation from which libraries could begin to experiment with advanced web services.

The work of both the EARL Consortium and the People's Network initiative can be considered as revolutionary changes akin to those described by Kathy Sierra (2005): each initiative at the national level propelled libraries into the digital environment, and more quickly than if they were to implement individually at their own pace. And this is not just down to the technological infrastructure, but more importantly to the creation of content through the digitisation programme. Libraries not only digitised documents and artefacts, but the programme required them to create webpages and learning materials around them. All together, British libraries provide an excellent example of the results of incremental and revolutionary change.

A hierarchy of library online implementation

Level 0: being there – getting and staying on the web

Libraries at this level represent themselves online through static webpages and some access to in-house or third-party services (catalogues, indices, abstracts and other reference resources). Communication with the public is asynchronous, through e-mail or web forms. Members of the public are able to perform functions online (renew books, etc.); however, many of these services can be accessed offline, either by going into the library or over the phone. Although there is communication with the public, there is no collaboration or community-building online, indirect or otherwise. Web application cannot even be considered at level 0 of O'Reilly's Web 2.0 hierarchy: O'Reilly regards e-mail and IM as 'another whole class', in some senses belonging more to Web 1.0. Although to a certain extent I agree with O'Reilly in this distinction, see below on the role of e-mail-based technology used with a Web 2.0 ethos.

These services and information are basically one way, from librarian to user. They can be provided offline (over intranets, local area networks, via caches, etc.). The value gained from being on the web, for libraries, is ease of access for those library users becoming more dependent on information from the web, for instance the housebound, those who work when the library is open and, critically, those already dedicated library users who are conducting more and more of their business and leisure online.

Although this is 'the historical level', where public libraries started about 15 years ago, there are still libraries more comfortable with offering 'pre-packaged information', largely database-driven, where little input online is required by themselves or the public. It is a more passive delivery of information, replicating the traditional, perhaps stereotypical, role of physical libraries.

For British public libraries, aside from the digitisation projects funded by the government, library pages remained relatively static for a time. There was certainly no promise of interactivity or user-generated content; in fact, some libraries were reluctant to provide contact e-mail addresses for a time, either because they did not have them or because they were not accustomed to handling business in this way. In most cases only postal addresses were provided. But this was the nature of quite a few Web 1.0 pages; it was all about directional, locational or service description information, all going one way from librarian to user.

While this little bit of UK public library history is useful to show how far public libraries have come in such a short time (especially in the sense that they are usually more ahead of the technology curve than any other local government department), that many libraries are comfortable at this level requires some consideration. I would be inclined to include at this level the libraries using Web 2.0, but in such a way that the services have nothing to do with user content creation or community-building (for example, the use of RSS, blogs and micro-blogs simply to post announcements about library events). This may be using the technology, but the ethos and the unique functionality afforded by the software has not been realised. There are various reasons for not moving to the next level, having to do with capacity, technology and legal restraints. In order to take advantage of the new service orientation that is often demanded from the use of the more advanced web tools, there would have to be a change, perhaps in the corporate culture, to allow for more risk, innovation and interactivity in web-based services. Because ultimately it is down to corporate will, maybe government will, to push forward to the top level.

Level 1: the Web 2.0 frontier

Library online services at this level include synchronous communication with users, such as chat and text. This is an important step, in that librarians are using their web presence not as a passive means of transferring information, but as a place to conduct a real-time exchange with users. Libraries at this level are also uploading user-generated content, albeit using such e-mail-based technologies as web forms. While the technology itself is not Web 2.0, and there is still no collaboration or community-building as such, some of the Web 2.0 ethos of users creating content is present. The two versions presented of the Bedfordshire Libraries website (Figures 4.1 and 4.2) represent the progress made by libraries in the past ten years. Where the two links in the first version of

Figure 4.1   Bedfordshire Libraries pre-history, circa 1997

Figure 4.2   Bedfordshire Libraries level 1, 2008

the page led to flat HTML pages of information (for the most part about the library), the links in the current version lead to a collaborative chat-based enquiry service, entries from a poetry-writing competition and stories written by members of the public. In fact, Bedfordshire provides online membership to those not from the county, with the only restrictions on use coming from licensing terms of certain resources, essentially eliminating the geographic boundaries of membership – rather forward thinking for an organisation ensconced in local government and dependent on its funding.

It's still Web 1.0, but...

Calling websites at one point Web 1.0 and at another Web 2.0 implies there was some kind of clear-cut demarcation between the two. At this level, it is important to understand that Web 2.0 did not supplant

Web 1.0 overnight, or indeed ever, as Web 1.0 still has its uses (see previous chapter for definition and use of Web 1.0); collaboration and user-generated content evolved gradually. At this level, webpages evolve towards the next level by opening more forms of communication, increasing real-time interaction between users and librarians: so not just e-mail or web forms, but also chat, instant or text messaging and discussion boards. An example of this move from asynchronous to real-time engagement with users is the People's Network Enquire, a UK-wide chat reference service, which evolved from a 1996 collaborative enquiry web-form service from EARL, 'Ask A Librarian'. This service has spawned a number of local interactive services, for homework help, discussions with authors and discussions with local authority chief executives. It was part of a suite of services, supported by the Museums, Libraries and Archives Council, to be delivered over the People's Network.

However, we cannot dismiss the impact of what some now consider a rudimentary form of communication, e-mail and e-mail-based software tools, in the evolution from the information to the user-generated web. Of course, in the beginning was e-mail, still a staple of online communication (and not just for losers, as I heard a conference speaker refer to it, relative to other, more dynamic forms of communication). E-mail has come a long way from the addresses on library websites, whose existence was promptly ignored. It is important to note that, if Web 1.0 is the information web where users go to receive information, the user-generated web began with people using Web 1.0 tools to talk over that information in communities of shared interest. E-mail has transformed a bit, in that its use has engendered communities using e-mail and e-mail-based technologies (web forms etc.) to search for information, meet other people with whom to share interests, ideas, advice, and in some cases to create and collaborate. The lowly web form, sometimes connected to a content management system, is not glamorous or whizzy, but can be an excellent tool to enable users to contribute content (see Stories on the Web case study).

An example of the web form in a Web 2.0 spirit is Gateshead Arts and Libraries Children's Book Award, launched in 2004. Originally there was no specific plan for this to be an online service; the award shortlist was promoted online but its primary activity, voting, was conducted via print. Having experimented online with discussion of books using forums, Gateshead then extended this use to online reviews and voting, which it found the children really loved (Figure 4.3). The award is now

Figure 4.3 Gateshead's Children's Book Award

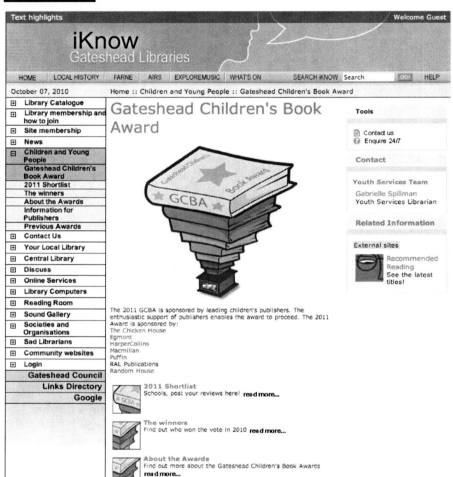

conducted solely online, an example of service development that was led by user demand. Comments and reviews posted on the web form appear immediately on the website (Figure 4.4). This is quite staff intensive for a defined period – there are no dedicated staff to manage the process, but the team responsible for the Children's Book Award have been trained to edit the website and take this responsibility on as part of their wider duties.

An e-mail-related technology especially instrumental in user communication and collaboration is the internet forum, message board

Figure 4.4 Gateshead's Children's Book Award comments

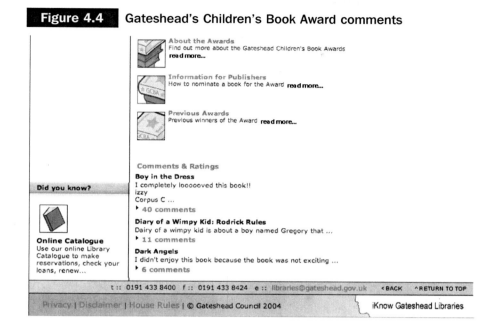

and mailing list. Although not considered as dynamic as other forms of communication, because it ties users to specific websites and PCs, this technology is still popular and the groups are considered a source of information and expertise in themselves: when people are looking to make purchases – cars, appliances, houses – these sites are often used, even by those who don't make a contribution.

Often, communities are built around swapping or buying and selling goods. Everyone knows about eBay. But equally popular are the FreeCycle communities around the UK, where people give goods and sometimes services away for free. (I got my oak dining-room table from Fenland FreeCycle!) It works on an e-mail alert each time a new message is posted. Other web forums do require users to log in to view messages; however, some sites offer e-mail notification and an aggregation of messages from the forum.

While communities of librarians have embraced this technology, it has been also used as a means of communicating with the library public. Kent County Council Libraries and Archives has hosted a libraries and archives discussion forum since 2002, and includes reading, family history and art groups, with good examples of discussion among users and not just between librarians and users.

As challenging as the use of asynchronous technology is for libraries, it is still not Web 2.0. It is right at that frontier where real-time and close-to-real-time communication lead to real-time creation. The move from Web 1.0 to Web 2.0 is the move from giving (information) to library users to those users giving back – or more to the point, sharing with librarians and other users.

Libraries at this level are usually more able to take the risks and do the necessary negotiating with IT departments required for the implementation of new technology. Adopting real-time communication mechanisms has been made easier for UK public libraries with such collaborative services as the People's Network Enquire, which takes into account concerns regarding capacity and IT security. Those that have experimented with user-generated content, especially among young people, have been motivated by how the services have been transformed online. However, libraries at this level have not yet risked experimenting with more advanced tools, and may still be reluctant to do so because of the implications of allowing users loose on services and sites.

Case study: Stories from the Web

Managed by Birmingham Libraries, hosted by UKOLN (www.storiesfromtheweb.org/).

> Books are definitely not doomed... Just because the internet has taken over the adult world doesn't mean it will affect ours. We, as kids, can live in the present while thinking of the future and reading about the past, it makes life so much more interesting. Also, reading gives people a chance to dream, to imagine themselves being somebody who they are not, in some world other than our own. It allows the imagination to stay intact even as you grow older. I don't think anybody would be wanting to give up on readig [sic] and on books any time soon because they are too important to our culture and to education, logic and most importantly to having fun. (Discussion list contribution from the website)

Reading and creating online

Any online service that can elicit this kind of enthusiasm about reading and books has got to be doing something right! Stories from the Web is an excellent example of a sustainable, collaborative library service operating on a national scale according to the Web 2.0 ethos of user-created content and communities before Web 2.0 technologies even existed. The service has continued to increase library and community participation, as well as upgrading its technology through the use of webcasting and streaming media, to promote reading, writing and creative activities by the main users of the site, children and young people.

Stories from the Web began life as a project in 1997, led by Birmingham Libraries in partnership with the library services of Bristol and Leeds, as well as the UK Office for Library and Information Networking (UKOLN), which hosts the website. The collaboration developed an entirely web-based community of readers and writers among children. The service includes activities designed for ages 0–7, 7–11 and 11–14. The website both supports and is the conduit for the activities: children can read extracts from fiction and poetry works on the site, which are usually packaged with creative writing activities. The results of these activities, including original stories and drawings, are displayed in the 'gallery' and form a permanent archive on the site.

The service is sustained by subscriptions paid by the over 30 library authorities currently participating at the time of writing. Families are registered for the service, and initially children were introduced to the site through book clubs, run weekly for an hour and a half each session. Original participation was encouraged through libraries where children signed up for the service after an application process. Parental consent was required at one time for participation in the clubs, but not for passwords or to upload stories and images to the site. However, if individual libraries participating in the service require parental consent for web use in general, then they apply this policy with Stories from the Web as well. Acknowledgement from the contributors that the work is their own is required; however, the only information available about an individual child is first name, age and locality. Any family names or other detailed information are removed before uploading.

Overall, not only did the project provide proof of concept for libraries delivering online services, but it also demonstrated that those services could raise the level of traditional library offerings. Findings from the original project report revealed that children involved with the service used the library more often and borrowed more books than they had before joining.

The challenges of delivering a web-based service

The technology

As UKOLN hosts the website, the service has not had the usual challenges faced by UK libraries dealing with local government internal or third-party IT departments, some of which have outright banned the use of Web 2.0 and other interactive tools, mostly out of fears over security and liability. Although this is not the case for Stories from the Web, the partnership has yet to implement Web 2.0 software that would enable the children to create content or discuss books in a live setting online. There are plans for a blog and a forum for the revamped staff page to be launched in 2010. The blog will be for the staff area, which can only be accessed by adults. After consultation with young people the libraries are considering a blog for the redesigned 11–14 site. However, this will be a fully moderated blog so no comments would go live until viewed by the Stories from the Web team, and edited if required – in effect this will make it as safe as the rest of the site.

For now, most contributions are of an asynchronous nature: children do write comments, but using web forms. This kind of technology allows for the moderating of all work before it is uploaded to ensure the safety of the site for its child users. The service has recently implemented streaming audio/video of authors reading their work and encouraging children to read and write. Although UKOLN hosts the actual site, participating libraries are required to have the latest version of the software necessary to access this and other content. Ensuring that children across library authorities have the same access to the site and its features is a challenge, as UK public libraries depend upon other departments or in some cases third-party companies to maintain their hardware, software and web content. What this means in practice is that while one library authority may be able to upgrade all its computers to the appropriate version of Flash, say within weeks, another authority may take months. So while children in the first authority may be able to view the author videos in a library setting, children in the second cannot.

Legal liabilities

The service administrators have addressed two main legal considerations through the Birmingham County Council legal department: copyright and data protection. The legal department has written the copyright permission form, used for every literary extract that is featured.

Moreover, the service has a good working relationship with around 40 publishers which have given generic permissions.

The second legal consideration involved the use of children's content and personal details. Although parents were required to give the initial permission for participation and display of content, the children in the act of uploading their material were required to give their consent before the content could be displayed. Initially, children gave their permission online by opt-in, but they didn't really understand the concept and its implications. Consequently, permission now operates on an opt-out basis. In addition, the content is monitored by the service administrators, and personal data are removed or names are changed.

The legal department did query what problems could result once the children had grown up and challenged the inclusion of their content.

Staff participation

Generally, staff benefited from participation in the service by gaining more confidence in their IT skills. The confidence came about, though, after the challenge of trying to develop a training programme across multiple library authorities. The training often took up much staff time, both for those being trained and those developing, preparing and delivering the sessions. Also, that part of the original project implementation where the children were using the computers presented in microcosm what was to become a source of frustration for libraries universally: the continuous requirement for technical troubleshooting by librarians.

Concluding remarks

Stories from the Web is one of those services on the borderline between Web 1.0 and Web 2.0 implementation. The technology used is still predominantly Web 1.0, but in terms of the ethos of the service it is an early example of O'Reilly's level 2, as it is a service that can only be used online (although in conjunction with offline activities). One of its primary objectives is to be delivered over the network, which maximises the participation it is seeking to attract. Moreover, and what makes it clearly an example of early social networking, it illustrates Leadbeater's level 2, instrumental collaboration, in that the main goal of the service is collaboration, to foster reading and writing, as well as the creation of original work.

In fact, the Stories from the Web project identified 'building online community' as one of its main objectives, placing considerable value on children's participation – their opinions of the site, books they wanted to read and their thoughts about the web. In this way, the Stories partnership built a participatory framework from the beginning, not only in terms of the technology it employed but also by carefully targeting and building its community of users, providing children and their families with motivation for participating. That the technology was new and different for the children at the time of launch was motivation enough for using the website; ease of use ensured that they did not quickly become disenchanted with that part of the service.

Information based on interviews with Doreen Williams and Debbie Mynott from Birmingham Library and project reports, including Everall et al. (2001).

Level 2: experimenting with Web 2.0

At this level, library online services include opportunities for members of the public to communicate with each other through the use of not only such Web 1.0 tools as forums but also Web 2.0 technology such as blogs, micro-blogs, podcasts, RSS and photo sharing (at this level I would exclude video and music sharing, as they would require a bit more staff input and capacity, as well as assumption of risk, even at an experimental level). Moreover, some libraries are experimenting with social networking services such as Facebook and MySpace. Depending on the manner of implementation, libraries are either at Leadbeater's level 1, in that they are using the tools as passive means of communicating information, events and activities, or level 2, where the use of photo and social networking tools indicates a heightened interest in a more social forum for content and collaboration with communities of interest. Tools such as blogging software are often used passively, no more than a digital bulletin board or newsletter, or in some cases demonstrate 'instrumental collaboration' (see the Gateshead case study below for concurrent examples of levels 1 and 2) in that they are used for a specific purpose, such as a means for a project team to interact.

Generally (and there are exceptions), libraries simply experimenting with Web 2.0 tools use them more for staff purposes or as a means of communicating news, essentially communication going one way. Examples of Web 2.0 library services, such as those to be found on sites like the UK wiki 'Libraries and Web 2.0', demonstrate that this is the most frequent type of usage. For example, while Facebook and MySpace library pages represent a willingness to raise profiles in new places and bring services where users (and probably mostly non-library users) are, whether they be experimental or live pages, and sometimes it is difficult to judge which, they take the format of a typical branch library page – which for most libraries are very much slimmed-down and static versions of main library websites. In the previous chapter it was demonstrated that there was nothing wrong with using these services as branch library pages, but librarians should ensure that they are indeed virtual branches which call for the exploitation of all the network and software functionality in order to liberate them from geographic boundaries. Predominantly on these social networking sites, traditional library services offered by UK libraries, such as the catalogue, are accessed via a link to the corporate library site, so no searching is offered directly from the social networking page. A quick trawl through various public library Facebook and MySpace pages reveals little input from users (and not many registered as friends or fans). Invariably, the pages are maintained by one tireless library staff member doggedly logging events and announcements, thus providing most of the traffic on the page.

Nor does there seem to be much use of other Web 2.0 applications on the pages or any exploitation of the virtual environment. For example, one library posted an announcement for a reading group that met *in the library*. This is an example of a missed opportunity to exploit the unique functions of these social networking sites: to create a virtual community out of a group of readers whose main form of communication would be the page itself. In an another example, while the library had experimented with videos on the Facebook site, there is an indication right on the webpage that it had only been publicised to the library sector, even though it appeared to be a video targeted at users. There is no real user input on the page, only about 12 fans, so essentially it represents a lesser-functioning version of the homepage within Facebook. So these libraries cannot really be said to be using Web 2.0; they are simply experimenting with the tools, according to traditional patterns of access on their main websites.

The excuse might be that 'We're just experimenting!' However, because there is so much scepticism about these tools, not just within libraries but also across government departments, it really has become a requirement of libraries to experiment responsibly (for more on experimentation, see Chapter 5). After all, a major reason for experimentation is to judge potential success. I suppose if the success factor is just the simple fact of being able to create a Facebook page or

Twitter account then these services, as well as the web itself, are littered with successful pages! (And we all know the frustration of coming upon pages that are useless because they have not been updated in a long time and are neglected by creators and users alike. There really is enough litter on the web!) I hope we have all been disabused of the notion that the minimal use of technology will have the optimal effect of augmenting usage and changing the library profile. Even an experiment needs a business case, even if it contains simply a list of critical success factors.

For the challenge at this level is to be open to using the additional functionality of the tools to attract new users in new ways. It is not enough to create services where use and expectation are minimised from the very beginning because of fear of risk, lack of capacity or concerns over legality. None of these things should matter if libraries set the parameters for success from the start, even in experimentation, and cut the service cloth so to speak in order to be successful even within their limitations. It is not clear whether libraries at this level are not taking up this challenge in any great number because of these factors. It is clear, however, that they will not be able to go on to the next level without the foundations of a good business case that resolves fears, manages not minimises expectations, and thus ensures as much of a success as possible in taking the leap.

Case study: Gateshead Arts and Libraries – a tale of two blogs

It is no exaggeration to say that Gateshead Libraries has usually been at the forefront of new technology implementation among UK public libraries. As mentioned above, it was hosting and maintaining its local authority website when most UK public libraries were just beginning to think about their own. Over the years, Gateshead was the first UK public library to implement a chat reference service and run a successful online book award for children (see above), and currently it is working on a variety of Web 2.0-based services.

Gateshead began experimenting with blogs in 2001. First, it developed a general-purpose blog combining library news with events and reading topics. Soon after, it also launched a blog that was specifically linked to the Lottery-funded 'Farne' project dedicated to raising the profile of Northumbrian music online, as well as providing an information hub for folk music. The blog served as a promotional tool for the project, and examples of content which would eventually be found in the wider archive were added regularly to create interest in the final website when it launched. The blog hosted by Gateshead was in operation for the two-year duration of the project, and was successful in gaining comments and contributions from the folk music community, who had already embraced use of the web as a networking tool. The Gateshead project team quickly discovered that there was a well-established online folk music community, and once its members learned about the project, interest increased.

When comparing the two blogs, it became clear to Gateshead that the Farne-related blog was more successful as a promotional tool, not just because it was targeted at a specific project audience, but because the project as a whole offered something of interest to a wider, well-established online community. This particular community blogged regularly and used other tools as a means not only of communicating, but also of promoting music. The Farne blog, seen as the prime marketing tool for the project, was embraced by the project team. The general-purpose blog had a wider, albeit Web 1.0, purpose: it was used for promoting events to the public, the promotion of new resources to library users and staff, and to prompt general discussion around library use. As such it did not appeal to a defined online community and did not fall to specific library staff to maintain. The wider library blog was seen as an extension of traditional marketing methods. While it was less successful than the Farne blog in prompting discussion and promotion online, it marked a useful starting point in asking library staff to consider online marketing alongside other activities and introducing them to the use of new online tools.

We have already seen that a participation framework is intrinsic to the success of a Web 2.0 service; Gateshead's Farne blog demonstrates that the user population do not always need to be developed by the library. Sometimes all that is required is the identification in advance of existing communities willing to participate.

Concluding remarks

The Gateshead example demonstrates the difference between using technology for its own sake as opposed to using technology that fits and supports a specific service. In the majority of cases, the first will meet with failure. The second has a better chance of success, as there is the unique selling point as well as an identified audience or customer base for the service.

Gateshead's librarians emphasised the importance of staff support and training to the success of implementing such new technology as Web 2.0 tools. Gateshead recognises that it will never have the luxury of dedicated staff to drive forward use of technology. Instead, managers encourage and support staff who are interested in technology to develop Web 2.0 initiatives alongside other duties. Where this can fail is when initiatives become dependent on personalities – some level of mainstreaming needs to be incorporated so that as staff change roles the work continues to be embraced. The level of staff commitment required for implementing Web 2.0 tools is an ongoing issue not just for Gateshead but for all public libraries.

Information based on an interview with Rachel Peacock from Gateshead Arts and Libraries.

Level 3: new libraries, new communities

Libraries at this level have taken up the challenge not just to use the Web 2.0 technology, but also to engage in the Web 2.0 ethos that encourages collaboration and community-building, and more importantly supports user-generated content as its foundation. This involves not just using the tools in a more active manner, but using them in such a way as to foster a creative environment, whether it be librarian or user creativity. Primarily, libraries are using tools such as wikis and social networking services as a way to target and involve those who are not traditionally library users. As the librarians at Gateshead learned, the way to accomplish this goal is to identify the community, create a service and use the technology to reach and engage that community. Of course, as illustrated by the social catalogues in Darien and Oakville in the previous chapter, these libraries are also willing to take the ultimate risk of allowing users to 'co-create' the library.

Case study: Portsmouth City Council Library Service

The Book Case (www.thebookcase.wetpaint.com); the Teen Wiki (www.teenreadinggroup.wetpaint.com).

The Book Case is cool. It allows you to have your own opinion towards things, and lets you look at other people's opinions. As I like reading, it is cool you can discuss books. Thumbs UP! Keep it UP! (Comment from online discussion group)

An important part of the mission of any local government authority is to encourage more public participation in cultural activities and events. Portsmouth City Council (UK) is one such authority, and the library has developed the ideal service to match this objective: The Book Case. The Book Case is a public-facing wiki, supporting book lovers and readers over 18 years of age in the search for good books, and encouraging them to exchange their views and experiences online through reviews and recommendations. 'Writers' are encouraged to create and maintain their own interactive pages, sometimes focusing on specific genres, such as 'ladies who lunch'. From the beginning, writers included library staff as well as online users, encouraging a truly collaborative environment. The Teen Wiki was developed to support the teen reading groups in Portsmouth and is moderated by the teens themselves. It includes such activities as book discussions and the writing of a collaborative novel. As an example of developing a service to attract an experienced community of web users, the Teen Wiki community has participants from around the world.

Officially launched in June 2007 at Portsmouth Central Library, The Book Case had the support of popular authors and reading groups across Portsmouth. Like Stories from the Web, it aimed from the outset to encourage reading and writing, as well as build a community based on staff and public collaboration. In this respect, it exemplifies Leadbeater's instrumental collaboration in that it contributes especially towards the goals of the library's literacy development strategy. It is also exploits Web 2.0 technology to support a ready-made framework for participation through its Teen Wiki.

The wiki format allows direct engagement between librarians and users, as well as among users themselves. The specific software chosen, WetPaint, was free of charge and had been used by a number of other organisations. Moreover, implementing a specifically Web 2.0 technology allowed the library to address a number of corporate and service issues, including exploiting the expertise and enthusiasm of staff and readers alike, dealing with restrictive corporate IT guidelines and embracing the spirit of Web 2.0/Library 2.0 as a means by which to transform public library service.

The full Web 2.0: not without its challenges

To a certain extent, the library understood the challenges that would have to be surmounted before taking on the full Web 2.0 experience. For instance, it was promoted to and had buy-in from senior management before implementation, and there was a comprehensive promotion campaign before the launch, involving roadshows and demonstrations to branch libraries and reading groups. Still, even with a good deal of preparation, problems did surface.

The technology

Portsmouth City Council IT, not unlike many local government IT departments, was proscriptive regarding the use of Web 2.0 on local government websites. In a sense, this problem is what made the wiki software, WetPaint, ideal for the library's purposes: it is a remotely hosted service, so using it would mean that The Book Case does not come under the auspices of corporate IT. The library was also able to customise the pages in a way that it was not at liberty to do with its corporate website. However, the remote site did not entirely resolve the issue with corporate IT, as there were still concerns about a remote site run by a council department that was not officially branded and governed by accessibility and impartiality standards. This issue remained despite the library branding the site as 'unofficial', thereby distancing the council from responsibility. However, because the contact details came from the council, the website would be perceived as a council product and therefore would have to adhere to the council's established rules. Much deliberation and negotiation within the council resulted in an agreement to allow the contact details as well as a link from OPACs to remain.

There were additional concerns with the technology and the remote hosting, including possible hacking of the site, ensuring continuity of service and the lack of a service level agreement as the software is open source. These and other concerns resulted in the development of a 'conditions of use' document (see below).

Staff involvement

Although the library was scrupulous in procuring senior staff support for the service, there was little initial effort in advocating across and down. As a result, there was a bit of resistance early on from staff, especially those in reader development, who felt that they were burdened with a new and strange service requiring extra work and responsibility. Generally, the degree of take-up by staff fell along the lines of traditional age divisions: older staff found the software and service orientation more threatening than junior members of staff. The library champions of the service realised that there might have been more acceptance by the staff if a working party had been set up at the same time as, or even before, staff were trying to win support from senior management.

Initially it was thought that the wiki would not be staff-intensive, because it was a site dedicated to user-generated content. However, in order to ensure quality, currency and content free from civil liability, contributions must be reviewed, which is time-consuming. For most of its online life the service has not had any dedicated staff, so managing it makes for extra responsibility.

Legal liability

Corporate IT was not the only department with concerns regarding the wiki. The issues raised by the legal department are shared by those with websites in the public and private sector alike, including the posting of defamatory or malicious material, undesirable third-party advertising and infringement of copyright. The council could protect itself from civil liabilities, such as libel and defamation, if participants signed a writers' contract. However, this solution would not necessarily work for the Teen Wiki, as those under 18 years of age cannot be held to contract. One of the ways Portsmouth has tried to maintain some control over writers external to the library is through a vetting process, where members of the public have to sign up to be a writer and complete a snail-mail agreement form, where standard personal and contact information is required, as well as an exchange with the library regarding the activities in which they would participate and what level of support they would need. This last bit of information is intended as a deterrent to improper use, as well as a signal to the writer that the library is actively engaged in supporting the service. There are also conditions of use posted on the site which address some of the concerns about legal liability (Figure 4.5).

Concluding remarks

Portsmouth's experience with the wikis serves as an excellent example of many of the crucial issues which arise when implementing a service that

Figure 4.5 The Book Case conditions of use

Apply to be a Writer   Share this   Report page

Conditions of Use

By registering to use this wiki you agree to the following:

1. Portsmouth City Council takes no responsibility for the content or security of any external site or third party advertising, whether accessed via this site or otherwise.
2. Site users are responsible for their own postings. Whilst we delete comments that are offensive, libellous, 'off-topic' or spam, readers may occasionally find some comments controversial. The responsibility for the posting lies with the poster himself/herself and not with Portsmouth City Council.
3. The Book Case banner and Portsmouth City Council logo is © Copyright Portsmouth City Council under Section 17 of the Copyright, Designs and Patents Act 1988. For further information please navigate to http://www.portsmouth.gov.uk/HomePage/copyright.html.
4. Please do not publish any personal information about yourself such as email addresses or telephone numbers. This is for your own protection. Portsmouth City Council cannot accept any responsibility if you disregard this request. For further advice about online safety please navigate to the Report Abuse page.
5. By using this site, you confirm that you are 13 years of age or older.
6. Writers must be 18 years of age or older. We recommend that younger people apply to be writers on the teen wiki www.teenreadinggroup.wetpaint.com.
7. The Administrator reserves the right to refuse writer requests without explanation.
8. Users must agree to not break copyright law and guarantee that all their work is their own.
9. Users must not post libellous or inappropriate content. They understand that any libellous content may be subject to legal action.
10. Users agree that the Administrator of the Book Case has the right to delete or modify any content and that the Administrator has the final say in what is regarded as appropriate content.
11. Users must understand that any content that is in anyway deemed to be a form of harassment or in breach of equalities legislations WILL be reported to the appropriate body.

combines Web 2.0 technology with user-generated content. Some of these issues can be resolved by simply using remotely hosted websites, although local government may still require such documents as writers' contracts and user agreements so that risk can be minimised for all parties. But some are endemic to the web, such as the posting of offensive material and copyright violation, and have yet to be resolved as the nature of the issues themselves is evolving.

Portsmouth used an existing participation framework, including its reading groups and some library staff buy-in, essentially to launch a revolutionary service at a local level. The librarians could have implemented a wiki through incremental steps, perhaps beginning with staff as an internal experiment, or as a pilot with a narrowly defined user group for a limited time. However, they launched a live service, knowing most of the risks, minimising them where possible, but ultimately realising that a leap would be necessary if a service of that type were ever to get off the ground.

Information based on interview with Pat Garrett from Portsmouth City Library and service documentation.

Conclusion

Applying O'Reilly's (2006) hierarchy to the evolutionary stages of public libraries online helps libraries to understand where they are in Web 2.0 development, where they want to be and, through some key case studies, how to get there. In addition to reinforcing the lessons from the previous chapters, such as building or identifying the participation framework, the examples from this chapter demonstrate that in the digital environment, progress, improvement and properly managed development are crucial to public library visibility: libraries afraid to take risks may find their roles only at the margins of information delivery. The case studies not only illustrate this challenge and some solutions, but reinforce the foundation of good business and service planning.

Create a new corporate ethos

Although Web 2.0 technology can be implemented along a sliding scale that is dictated by capacity and budget, complete implementation involves not just the use of the technology but a change in library and the wider corporate ethos, working practices and relationship with the public. Libraries contained within a centralised corporate and technology structure can achieve little without the knowledge (in terms of Web 2.0 this is often lacking) and support of corporate IT and legal departments. In the example of Portsmouth, the case to be made was taken all the way up to the chief executive's office and involved other directorates, such as communications.

Start with a participation framework

Adopting the technology does not stop at implementation, then: the library must marry the technology to an already existing community of web users, or else dedicate its time and resources to creating a community itself. Of course, it saves time and even money if a library can connect up with a group of dedicated users online who understand the values of social networking. If this is not the case, then it is imperative for success, and especially if success has to be demonstrated within a short period of time, to build that community and educate it about the benefits of interacting online. Both Gateshead and Portsmouth illustrate how a service can take off if a community takes an interest: with

Gateshead the folk music people, and with Portsmouth teens with an interest in writing. For Stories from the Web, children with a specific interest in the web and reading provided a ready-made community.

Avoid the blame game

Otherwise, the failure cycle will occur: no one will use the technology, the library will blame the technology, the library will not adapt to Web 2.0 'because it doesn't work', the library will try another new technology, no one will use it, etc. etc.

Build a new communication and information paradigm

The old information relationship with the public – the library provides the information – must either give way or be augmented by a new paradigm: the public creates content and gives it to the library, or to other members of the public, via the library website.

Know and minimise risks

Because this paradigm is currently fraught with legal and IT complications, libraries and local governments must ensure quality and protect themselves from liability. And the concerns may not be related to current liability: in at least one example above, the legal department was concerned about future liability, in terms of how what is agreed now by parents for their children may be challenged by these same children when they are adults. In quite a few cases this does require that the library educate the other departments (creating the corporate ethos), and, as is the case in most attempts to educate, expect that there might be initial and indeed prolonged resistance.

In the end, it comes down to planning and risk assessment. However, there is a point where planning and fear of risk have to stop, and service delivery has to begin. Some of the learning, probably quite a bit of it with the new collaborative paradigm, will happen along the way, as Fichter (2006) points out:

> Radical trust is about trusting the community. We know that abuse can happen, but we trust (radically) that the community and

participation will work. In the real world, we know that vandalism happens but we still put art and sculpture up in our parks. As an online community we come up with safeguards or mechanisms that help keep open contribution and participation working.

Notes

1. I acknowledge that Leadbeater's levels of collaboration do not necessarily represent a hierarchy in the sense that O'Reilly's do. However, there is a value to purposeful collaboration that is of benefit to a whole community as opposed to just the individual.
2. In the UK, public library websites are included within the local government websites, as one among many local government services. Consequently, their website software and hardware are administered through a corporate IT department, which can often be outsourced to a third-party company. Its responsibilities include installation and overseeing currency and security. Often libraries trying to implement new technologies must make a business case to this department for approval.
3. EARL had over 160 local library authority partners, equating to 75 per cent of all local authorities in the UK. For more about EARL the best source is the EARL webpage, which can be accessed through the Internet Archives' Wayback Machine: http://web.archive.org/web/20001208013400/www. earl.org.uk/partners/index.html. Note that an alternative way of looking at this page is to go to the Internet Archive page (http://web.archive.org) and then enter the EARL address into the Wayback Machine (www.earl.org.uk).

Part IV
'Tilling the soil, seeding the ideas': the Web 2.0 business case

5

Introducing Web 2.0

Moreover improvements were being incorporated as fast as they could be conceived. 'The design they've come up with... changed 10 times before they delivered... We're inventing and creating at critical path... I've got guys trying to release things before they are actually invented.' (Rauch, 2008)

In the fast-paced commercial environment, taking risks and launching before being fully prepared are often mandatory. However, this is not to say that there is no preparation, no planning, and most importantly no expertise upon which the first two are built. Much creativity and a number of hours precede any product release. Even though library service development can progress at a relatively more leisurely pace, the commitment to preparation is as critical.

In the previous chapters we have seen many examples demonstrating different approaches to Web 2.0 implementation in libraries, some in conjunction with service development and some not. These examples can be organised according to different implementation entry points.

The experiment level

Here librarians try out some of the more basic tools with internal colleagues (staff blogs, for example), or a bit more publicly but with no fanfare or publicity: one day the library's not twittering, the next day it has an account. One brave person in the library usually embarks on the experiment, and tries to keep things going in addition to full-time responsibilities. For the most part, little thought is given to outcomes or critical success factors. Often the rush comes solely from the sense of accomplishment in just setting up the Facebook page or putting those photos on Flickr. And so, when asked by the inevitable survey-takers if they have tried Web 2.0, they can proudly point to their Facebook or Flickr pages.

But I am not going to let librarians experimenting with the tools off that lightly – unless, right after they have proven to themselves that they know all there is to know about Facebook, they immediately delete the page or else go on to one of the other levels. It is not just that inactive pages and websites are a nuisance to the rest of us, not just that it is digital littering, but it shows little awareness of the implications of the digital footprint. For even experimentation should have a purpose, if only to learn about the software (in which case see 'delete the page').

And remember to alert the few interested users to the temporary nature of the service, and then take it down or archive it once the experiment is over. The exasperation of users when they are trying to access a service much out of date is not a reaction to be encouraged.

Proof of concept or pilot level

This can be considered part of experimentation or not, depending upon how seriously the library regards the undertaking, which is often indicated by how many staff participate, how much time is allocated and how much the public is involved. Experimentation which is not solely for learning purposes (in which case the blog or Flickr account is deleted...) should progress to this level. At this level there should be some concrete objectives and outcomes which define success or failure, and the library should be addressing some of the more difficult issues identified in the case studies of the previous chapters. In other words, proof of concept is not just about whether the technology works: that can be assessed at the experimentation level, especially as most Web 2.0 tools are centrally hosted, third-party software and do not require local troubleshooting as with catalogue implementation. More importantly, it is whether the more human issues, such as liability, security and safety, can be resolved and risks minimised. As demonstrated in The Book Case example, these issues can be aggravated with third-party and especially open source software tools and websites without terms and conditions. Librarians should be particularly aware of the terms and conditions (or lack of them) on these sites when experimenting or testing with public participants.

And remember to alert the few interested users to the temporary nature of the service, and then take it down or archive it once the experiment is over. The exasperation of users when they are trying to access a service much out of date is not a reaction to be encouraged. (Yes, it sounds like a mantra, and should be one for any service provider in the private or public sector.)

Live service level

Here the library is fully committed to running the service and has also developed the policies that address risks and other issues. Starting at the proof of concept level is an important entry point before going immediately into a live service precisely because it gives the library space and time to work out technical and human issues. Also arising from the proof of concept level is the necessity of establishing critical success factors and regularly evaluating the service against these. An evaluation bypass because a library is only at the beginning stages is not good enough in the current digital and budget environment.

Business case and participation framework

None of these levels of implementation will work unless preceded by a foundation that includes two key elements: a strong business case and a participation framework. The first is required even at the experimentation level, where playing around with the various software and services is not considered an end in itself but the beginning of progressing through the levels. The amount of detail for the business case can be adjusted at each level, which means that while a full-blown case might not be necessary at the experiment level, for example, some basic objectives and critical success factors should be established to provide the foundation for other levels.

A participation framework is required at all levels with no exception – the most successfully implemented Web 2.0 software and services (employed for Web 2.0 and not Web 1.0 outcomes) are all about participation. The figure for catalogue traffic on the library websites mentioned in Chapter 3 – about 80–90 per cent of all the traffic on the sites – begs the question: how did libraries achieve this success rate for one service? The answer is pretty clear: there was already a motivation for users to participate – they wanted to find and check out books – and so there was already a participation framework in place. But libraries do not have it so easy with creating services from Web 2.0 tools, and as we have seen in previous chapters the major reason for failure is because they have not provided a motivation, a reason to participate, and as a result there is nothing upon which to build a participation framework, or even a service.

And one of the key issues to be explored during the evidence-gathering phase of the business case, and resolved to form an objective for the service, is the decision between creating something that will institute change by increment or change by revolution. In other words, will the library start with registering on Twitter, maybe just following awhile and then building gradually to create a public service, or will it use LibraryThing for Libraries, totally revamping the nature and purpose of its major online presence, with all the preparation and promotion required to make a success of it?

Building the (business) case

The concept

The commitment to successful service development begins with the business case. Librarians are always looking for model business cases, or rather that one dream business case, that magic bullet. The first thing to know is that there is no one perfect formula, just requirements that are as much about a library discovering what its objectives are and how it will set about achieving them as about getting senior management or whomever to hand over the approval and funding. I hate to get all New Age (which is actually pretty old by now), but the business case, or at least the evidence required to build it, should be a voyage of self-discovery for a library. Of course, if it is the first time a library has looked into its soul (and really it shouldn't be), it can be a frightening experience.

The second thing to know is that few of what are called business cases, especially in the public sector, actually are. In the commercial world, according to Andrea DiMaio (2009), 'a purpose is not a business case. It won't tell you how much money or time you are going to save, nor by how much you are going to improve in meeting certain quantitative goals.' And these last issues are precisely what online library competitors are thinking about, and which feature in their business cases. Library business cases talk about cost, but not in any analytical way and rarely in respect to return on investment (ROI). However, for UK central and local governments, enamoured of all things in the business community, every new technology requires a 'business case', no matter how devalued the term. Referring to a government sector client's initiatives, DiMaio observes:

> it occurred to me that almost none of those, including the most successful one, had any sort of solid business case behind. In some cases it was just a leap of faith (combined with the authority and clout of a leader to make it happen). In other cases there was just a general sense that greater transparency and collaboration could help, but there was no way to articulate the actual value. In other cases it was a response to the need to be seen as modern and up-to-date. Interestingly, all these can lead to either success or failure, which mostly depend on whether there is a sufficiently compelling purpose for those who are expected to participate.

Still, it's nice that libraries are not the only government departments a bit unclear about the concept. I will use the term here, but with perhaps a little less emphasis on ROI or rigorous cost analysis, especially as these are notoriously difficult to apply in the public sector. Accordingly, the format of an acceptable business case, as well as what elements to emphasise, will vary from library to library, so best first to check with senior management about appropriate formats.

The content

Nothing below will be new, or at least it shouldn't be, and, depending on individual formats, some parts may require more emphasis than others. The one overriding principle, derived from the library examples in this book, is that the business case should not begin with or be about the technology. Many of the successful services began with a community necessity: to promote reading or writing or computer literacy, for example. Some of the unsuccessful ones began with just the desire to have a Web 2.0 tool on their websites. It is a truism that many of the commercial web services considered cutting edge, like eBay or Amazon, did not begin with the technology, but with what the technology allowed these businesses to do, or more to the point what it allowed them to enable their customers to do. Essentially, we are talking about the unique selling point, which is a result of knowing the customer base, constituency, community, whatever, and matching what the library does with what they want. Of course, sometimes there is an element of creating something they don't know that they want until it has been created, which sometimes does work but is a fairly risky proposition for libraries. How does a librarian discover what the community wants or needs?

Step 1: do the research

Library, know thyself

Usually, research for a business case is all about the community and profiling, but I think there is a question before that, the answer to which may be derived from the most recent library mission statement or service plan and what changes might be made to it in the future. In the many resources I have consulted, the most critical first question is why? And if a library is far down the path of implementation, and this question has yet to be asked, then it must go back to the beginning and ask it. If the service is successful, a library might just get away with not asking it, but what happens when the service hits a rough patch? And, of course, if a service fails, it's pretty much too late to ask why it was launched in the first place. If the mission or all the strategy documents do not provide the answer, libraries must address this question of why, why this service, why this service with this technology (because, of course, we are not beginning with the technology, right?)? If the answer to the last question is because we don't want to be left behind or we will try anything to attract more users to the website, then I have another single-word sentence: don't. If librarians just want to experiment, in other words educate themselves about the new software, fine, but don't dress it up as service development. And don't be forced into the technology by all the Web 2.0 champions: be encouraged, be inspired, but not compelled.

It is important to admit up front that the public library cannot be all things to all people, although it tries to be in order to attract government funding. So it is crucial to make an honest assessment of the library mission, capacity and budget. This kind of information should be ready to hand, even if a little dusty, but what should also inform the process is the local government agenda. In the UK, quite a few libraries use local government priorities as a starting point for developing yearly objectives. For example, Portsmouth Library took its lead from a city council objective to involve more citizens in culture or cultural events. This may not be the case for every library, but it is worthwhile to discover what the priorities are in the city or town before taking a case to senior management: it may help managers to be able to talk it up to other departments, gaining more support for the service and library across the locality.

The community/participation framework

I would like to assume that libraries are committed to profiling on a regular basis (and not just when the government, or anyone, tells them to be), and that service development is not just a haphazard activity. If it is undertaken regularly, the information contained therein should still be useful and pretty much up to date. If it is not, then a community profile of some kind should be developed before any Web 2.0 implementation happens. Remember, social networking begins with the community, and if the library has no idea of the composition and requirements of its community, then it will not be successful in anything besides checking out books, if that. I do not say this lightly; I know that getting senior management and other colleagues receptive to the idea, setting up the process, collecting and evaluating the data, will require considerable effort and capacity. This may be so even when just an update to an existing profile is required.

However, with a bit of luck, sometimes a community presents itself, and if it is an especially web-savvy community, as in the case of the Gateshead blog, it is a great basis for a service that stands a chance of success and fulfils a need in the community. Gateshead's folk music project blog is an excellent example of this kind of serendipity. Other examples would be a community of local or family historians or gamers (as with Ann Arbor's blog). In the digital environment there is a bit of a cheat, or at least a short cut, to discovering communities: Google the community! Or Facebook or Twitter or MySpace it. Discovering where the various groups in a locality are meeting and what they are doing online should be part of community profiling nowadays, anyway. Find out where different groups of people from the community are currently hanging out on the web. Googling works, as does consulting community pages on library or local government websites (think of the mine of information on NorthStarNet). Approach them online – that's why they created the Facebook account. These social network services are a great way of connecting to and cultivating groups which may be interested in new services.

Ideally the service should be matched to a tangible community, and if it is already interacting on the web with larger communities, so much the better. However, community groups need not be web users: part of the service can be introducing them to the web, not just to demonstrate the information available online but also the methods for communication. Potentially, by helping them to build their own web space for interaction, the library can encourage them to create something that could be useful for them as a special-interest community, and perhaps for a wider group of users both inside and outside the locality. Working with an existing community will invariably provide a quick win for the service, which helps to build confidence in the technology.

Much more difficult for a library is to create a community itself. In the above two options there are already a unique selling point and a community, but where there is neither librarians are going to have to come up with both. In a sense, this is what Portsmouth has done: although its original selling point for The Book Case was derived from the council, the librarians refined it based on experience with more traditional reading groups. Still, it was not a foregone conclusion that they would be able to attract users and then be able to grow a disparate group of users into a community. On this score, the Teen Wiki was easier because it began with a group that was savvy and interested in content creation on the web. This type of 'need creation' may be best left to companies or other organisations that can throw a lot of money at sustained marketing campaigns and branding. At the very least, I would recommend librarians not take this on for their first foray into matching service-community-technology, as it would require quite a bit of capacity and budget. If it fails, it will leave a negative impression regarding a potentially useful technology with library staff, library administration, local government administration and most importantly the library's community, who just might think libraries are lamer than they originally thought because they don't know how to use the technology. Harsh words, perhaps, but I have been there with services half-heartedly developed with no sense of audience in mind. And it's always the technology that's to blame (see 'Avoid the blame game' in the previous chapter)!

The library community

This is an important part of business case evidence gathering, because it provides precedents from other libraries making a success of social networking services. In a sense, this book is part of library research, not the least because it provides the benefit of the experience and expertise of national and international peers. Moreover, the book is all about seeing not just what works, but what doesn't work or what's problematic even while working. Librarians can identify which models might be relevant to them, and then contact the librarians involved for more guidance. That the examples are relevant is important; no good using a better-resourced library's experience of a service as a model for implementation. Appropriate precedents, especially successful ones, are what make a business case persuasive.

The budget

There is no getting around the money question, but at this point I recommend that librarians not only have an idea of what is available but also of timing and disposition. By timing, I mean at what point in the budget year will a request for money be made? In the second quarter, when the reality of first-quarter cuts has sunk in (and everyone has had time to heal), there might be some money that could be freed up, or in the last quarter where libraries are either in spending-spree mode to allocate unspent funds or shut down, because they are waiting to see what will happen in the next budget year. By disposition, I mean whose sign-off is needed, and under what conditions or when might they be disposed to release funds. Assessing disposition is also about which managers and staff members will be likely to support the service, in both the financial and the advocacy senses.

Happily enough, quite a few web tools are freely available, but be aware of the hidden costs than can accrue from having to negotiate with local government legal and IT departments which may charge back for their services or advice. Also figure in staff time – for training, for participation. And, of course, there are the costs of regular marketing and promotion.

Return on investment, or rate of return (ROR), and potential revenue are key features of commercial business cases. Generally referring to the relationship between the amount of money gained or lost against the amount of money invested, this may appear to have little applicability at this level of service, especially when there is no cost associated with the software.[1] However, a version of this applies if the library is expending a great deal on capacity – number of personnel, time, consulting with other departments where charges may apply. In the examples of Stories from the Web, The Book Case and Teen Wiki, we saw a great deal of staff time taken up with training, promotion, vetting and monitoring. If any of these is solely an initial outlay of capacity, then it is relatively easy to demonstrate the overall benefit or return to senior management. However, if they are not only ongoing but likely to increase as the service is more successful, then some additional consideration needs to be accorded to both the fact and the implication of this type of investment, as well as how it can be presented in such a way as to gain approval. Of course, if a service is successful and raises the library profile, all excessive cost may be forgiven and maybe even additional staff and funds may be found (yes, it does happen).

If the reverse is the case, and after there have been a few rounds of the blame game, then someone must be brave enough to call a halt to the service before it haemorrhages more money and brings down more opprobrium on the library, especially from users (remember the 'exasperated users' mantra?).

Step 2: if we build it... The service

What is it for?

Presumably, the original work of identifying potential groups of interest has already been accomplished. So, now there is a community and some knowledge of its interests. But what does it want to do, or what does the library want to help it do? These two questions are related to the original 'why', but whereas the answers to that question described the library's motivation, the answers to these questions should reveal those of the community. Service development begins with an action: something wants to be done, should be done, needs to be done. If, as discussed above, an existing community is the starting point, making contact to determine what the library can offer is an important first step. For those groups on the web, it may be as easy as posting a message on a message board, or directly e-mailing the moderator. If the library has a community database, the details provided there should be a good starting point for contacting those not already on the web.

How will we do it?

Once the community's goals have been identified, a service plan should be drawn up, which will include the technology to support it. I do not mean to say that librarians cannot identify technology early on; if they do, they must make sure that the technology, whether it be a wiki or blog, is matched to the goals of the community and the manner in which it wants to communicate among its members and to those outside. Web 2.0 tools support an activity, and so an activity and, critical to success, people who want to engage in that activity should be identified. However, especially with Web 2.0, librarians often seem to base service development on the technology – they want to use it for anything, and that usually leads to failure. The contrast between Gateshead's two blogs illustrates the difference of uptake. So, really, it is at this point in building the business case that technology should be considered. Sometimes it is easy to put together a community and a technology. For instance, sad but true, everyone wants to appear on film, especially YouTube, nowadays. Putting kids and books together with film was inspired, yes, but also a bit predictable, hence StoryTubes.

The community, service and technology are the important building blocks of the service plan and the business case. Include in the community, though, the staff required to support it. The staff are a key partner in the endeavour: no matter how strong the first three building blocks, the service will fail if there is no support, facilitation, guidance and most importantly enthusiasm. Public libraries are usually critically understaffed, so coming to an early understanding of who will be available and when to support the service and the users must be an immediate concern. Some of this work should already have been undertaken in the research phase, but at this juncture, commitments must be made to the service. A considerable part of the service plan should also include staff training, on the technology and on supporting the public using the technology. Training usually interrupts staffing of core library service, so timescales and staff capacity should be assessed.

What happens if...?

No service is without risk: the more revolutionary, the riskier. And it is certainly true that social networking comes with some very specific risks that can have personal ramifications for users and legal implications for libraries. But there is no excuse for developing a Web 2.0 service blind to the risks; there are too many examples of what can go wrong, and destroy not only a service but an organisation's reputation. The Portsmouth case study provides an excellent example of the types of legal and other issues that arise with the use of Web 2.0 tools, and others have been mentioned throughout the book. Librarians should use these examples to generate a complete list, which is likely to include such issues as data protection, copyright and intellectual property rights, defamation and other types of civil liability, abusive behaviour, hacking, service level agreements, corporate or local government branding and reputation, network security, and protection and safety, especially of children. I'll talk about liaising with IT, legal and other departments below, but librarians should know the risks in advance of talking with these departments. Any business case worth its salt should demonstrate an awareness not only of the risks, but possible resolutions, providing examples of what other libraries have done in such cases. Libraries cited in this book have generally found resolutions to real and potential problems, but there are some extreme cases where Web 2.0 of any kind is forbidden across departments in specific localities, usually because some kind of abuse of service has either occurred or is anticipated. Developing any kind of service, no matter how innocuous, would be difficult in this kind of climate.

Happily not in this situation, Portsmouth has chosen to address some of these issues through the development of such documents as conditions of use and a writer's contract, as well as working towards some type of service level agreement with WetPaint. A serious consideration for any website owner publishing user-generated content is the responsibility for civil liability. Essentially, if a member of the public posts libellous or defamatory remarks on a library website, or violates copyright, the library can be held responsible and in some instances prosecuted for publishing the remarks. The Book Case's conditions of use, presented in the previous chapter, are a model for how these concerns can be addressed.

The software supplier in this case, WetPaint, protects itself from liability because it does not moderate use and publishes disclaimers on its site. It is to be acknowledged, though, that it would be a rare library which did not moderate material, as usually libraries and local governments have stringent quality compliance rules. The only way for libraries, and by extension local governments, to protect themselves is to moderate very closely and vet contributors, including having them sign contracts (of course, this in turn requires more staff time).

The writer's contract requests that writers accept and confirm in writing the elements set out in the conditions of use. Finalising a service level agreement with the supplier has proved somewhat more challenging, as the terms and conditions on the supplier's site make clear that it accepts little responsibility for what happens during the use of the software. So on points such as service resumption in the case of hacking, the supplier cannot make a commitment. WetPaint, as free software, probably exemplifies the approach taken by most free software suppliers

– essentially the user assumes the risk, in this case the library along with its community.

Personally, I have always been one to mind my digital footprint and guard my online privacy. Part of this concern is mercenary, I must admit: I refuse to wear most clothing with labels, especially T-shirts, as I figure if I am going to be a walking billboard then I want a cut of the profits (I'll make an exception for clothing like Levis, for instance, because everyone knows Levis by their cut, not their label, and they have been doing jeans forever). This attitude goes doubly for my personal data and my clicking on the internet. To a certain extent giving data is unavoidable, especially as an internet shopper. However, I am not going to gift-wrap my usage for companies to exploit through analysing clicks and psychometrics. It is one of the reasons why I am on the fence about social network services such as Facebook and Twitter, as well as blogging. This information is a gift to advertisers.

The point is that I am cognisant of these issues from a personal perspective, and also consider it the duty of librarians in the delivery of such services, especially to children, to ensure that they educate them about the risks, what they can do to protect themselves and, to a certain extent, the help that librarians, as professionals, can offer them. This is not overbearance: it is part of delivering an online service in the public sector. And there is enough published regarding internet advertising standards and internet crime to support the concerns. Raising awareness and, up to a point, acting as guardians for our public are the roles of librarians. And productive partnerships with legal and IT departments can help us fulfil these roles.

What does success look like?

I don't know which librarians find more difficult – budgeting or evaluating? My guess, based on what I have seen in services, is that it is evaluation every time. I have already noted what is essentially a mantra for Web 2.0 and evaluation: it's too early to tell; it's early days... Translation: we don't/can't/can't be bothered to evaluate. A major reason why there is no evaluation is because no critical success factors have ever been established, so there really isn't anything against which to base an evaluation. Also, librarians tend to think of evaluation as hits on the webpage, number of friends on Facebook, number of Twitter followers, etc., and then blame the software for not being able to supply exact data. But total numbers of users or hits or views are meaningless data, and as a critical success factor by themselves are unfocused. We have all seen people on Facebook with 500 friends – but these are friends-of-friends-of-friends-of-friends-of. It is a totally meaningless number – even McDonald's 'x amount served' has more meaning. Better to start with: everybody in the book club to be signed on as a friend to the Facebook page; a calendar of events to be published; one book discussion meeting a month to be held on Facebook; an agreed level of participation that is considered successful (maybe based on how many show up at the library for book discussions), etc. etc. It is this simple, and it is eminently measurable. There may be a quibble that some of these are more deliverables than data, but the successful completion of deliverables is how projects are evaluated, and these deliverables add up to outcomes – a thriving book discussion group on Facebook, which opens this library activity up to the housebound and physically challenged. This is what success looks like for our book discussion club, and it can be measured, whether the days are early or late.

Step 3: marshall the troops

It is important within the business case itself to identify support for the service, and in turn how the service supports the stakeholders. Essentially, this section or step should also be regarded as a checklist to ensure that key stakeholders have been identified and contacted before the business case is submitted. Not a few services have been blindsided by a group which either the librarians totally forgot or never even considered as a stakeholder. So many librarians are intent upon building a case to convince senior management that they forget about everyone else whose support they might need. Note that senior management do not come at the top of my list.

The community

A commercial business case would identify the customer base: who is going to consume the service and why. So a public sector business case should not only identify those members of the public who will be using the service, but also why they will use it, what it will do for them. Obviously, quite a bit of this evidence should have already been gathered in steps 1 and 2, but the benefits to the community bear repeating when librarians are identifying the overwhelming support from all quarters given to the service.

Staff

Note that I am placing colleagues, across and down, before senior management. For, after all, is the library manager actually going to do the dirty work to make a service successful? It's great to get the library director's approval, but if the rest of the staff think the whole thing is crazy, it's doomed. And it's not even the vocal ones who doom a service: when colleagues get all passive-aggressive, then a service really is doomed! All the case studies emphasise the importance of the support of staff and the creation of staff champions. There will always be negativity and fear among staff, especially in public libraries where a good portion of the staff may be lifers, so it is important to identify champions immediately among those who will be responsible for delivery. These champions should be enlisted in a programme designed to win over as many other staff members as possible. Be resigned to the fact that there will always be hold-outs, so make sure that service delivery marginalises these staff members as much as possible. They might be won over by success at a later date, but don't count on it.

Senior management

OK, we had to get to them eventually, and I don't mean to imply that they are not important. A good deal of effort may be necessary to encourage them to be if not enthusiastic, supportive, then at least not an obstacle to the service. This support is especially crucial where funding is involved. The business case should not be the first time a manager is hearing about a service: seeds can be planted quietly through informal conversations, during appraisals, in other words at times when a manager is most likely to be receptive. The evidence gathered as part of the business case should foster the support required, but of course there are managers resistant to pretty much anything where money is concerned. This is where psychology comes in. Portsmouth ensured that its wiki served the greater interest of the council, and if a librarian can connect a service to the wider agenda in such a way, thereby bigging up a manager to those higher up in the local government food chain, then everyone is a winner. It may be cynical, but if a service can support senior management in currying favour, raising the library profile or delivering larger programmes, then make that a focal point in the business case.

I'll tell you of the dream scenario: in recruiting library participants for a national service, we were told by one librarian that his manager said

'Sign us up! We'll get the money somehow!' Doesn't happen often, but when it does, it's library gold.

Other departments

The support from senior management and others senior in local government is a prerequisite in the education and support of other departments, such as IT, legal services, communications and public relations. Be prepared, especially with Web 2.0, to educate; it is likely that these departments have heard all the bad things, and as local government is generally a risk-averse culture, they have more than likely already put restrictions in place. Again, the Portsmouth case study is an excellent example of navigating around these departments. Librarians must know what the problems may be before approaching them, as well as some suggestions for minimising the risks and arriving at solutions that will please all parties. Perhaps getting them to partner a pilot where the main objective is to learn about the risks and how they can be resolved might give them a sense of control over the implementation. A business case that can make common cause with the interests of these departments, that can show a joined-up approach to public service delivery, is another kind of library gold.

Step 4: sell, baby, sell

Do not even think about it. Do not even consider submitting a business case that does not include a sustained and sustainable plan for promoting the service. Even a pilot that is large enough to warrant a business case needs to account for how users will be attracted and motivated to use the service. Usually librarians think about marketing/promotion/publicity as all the same thing, and that thing boils down to flyers, leaflets, posters at the beginning or launch of a service. But although they are interrelated, they are not all the same thing. For example:

- leaflets/posters/flyers are *advertising*, the library kind anyway
- articles and interviews in the media are *publicity*, although not controlled by the library as those reporting, journalists and broadcasters, will determine the message
- press releases and those branding messages written by the library for publication or broadcasting are *public relations*.

Who is in control of the message determines the difference between publicity and public relations. So a screaming headline in the local newspaper, 'Teen stalked on library wiki!', is publicity. 'The library teen wiki: where your children's safety online comes first', an article written by the library director for the local newspaper, is public relations.

All of the above is *promotion*, which is a set of activities that continuously keeps the product in front of the public. I swear the public relation pieces in the newspapers telling us how popular Twitter was are part of the reason why it is so popular now (yes, I do believe some of them were deliberate puff pieces). And the Iranian protests were excellent publicity for Twitter and Facebook. People started to regard it as not just a social tool, but a political one.

And all of these are part of *marketing*, but are not what defines marketing exclusively. Marketing includes providing incentives (such as contests with prizes, as in Oakville); the community profile is also part of marketing because the first principle is to identify potential customers. But most importantly, a marketing plan's objective is always to be aware of the customer's relationship with the product, or in the public sector, the community's relationship with the service. Do they get what they need from it? Has the community changed, requiring change from the service? Can the service be improved? How can value be added (more support? new technology?)? Some of this might sound like a service development plan. But I have seen relatively few service development plans where the focus is on the users in relationship to the service: tracking their requirements, their changes, what motivates them and how all of this will have an impact on the service and its growth. The outcome of the achievement of the marketing plan's objective should be growth. And so a business case for a successful service (that's part of the promotional aspect of a business case, the presumption of success) will include how the service is created – the service development plan – and how it grows – the marketing plan.

Another part of marketing is sales, and a library's first sales activity is the business case. The assembling of it and the key stakeholders and champions collected on the way are part of sales, as the librarian is personally cultivating support. But the crucial test of the service's saleability will be the reception of the business case by senior management.

I know it does not necessarily help to say that the business case, and such plans to be included as marketing and service development, will vary depending upon the level (experiment, pilot, live), local conditions such as mission, objectives, management priority and disposition, and the all-important budget and capacity. To my mind, all of this could matter but none of it really does. Because no matter how little is expected of a librarian looking to implement a service, there is no substitute for preparation. And preparation is knowing all the eventualities. And doing it anyway.

Business case best practice as exemplified in the case studies

- *Stories from the Web.* The development and ongoing delivery of Stories from the Web exemplifies some key points for a business case, including the importance of marketing, sustainability, partnerships and service tailored towards a specific community and according to library business priorities.

- *The Book Case.* The Portsmouth wiki provides an excellent model of such business case points as creating a service that is tailored to a specific community and according to library business practices; creating champions up and down the staff hierarchy; developing partnerships not just with service providers, but also with required local government departments; creating a sustainable service; managing training and staff capacity; and knowing the risks, minimising them when possible, but realising that a leap might be necessary or else the service will never get off the ground.

- *Gateshead's blogs.* The Gateshead experience with blogs illustrates important requirements for a successful business case and service, including unique selling point, target audience, targeted marketing, technology supporting service and staff champions.

Notes

1. However, there is the concept of the Social Return on Investment (SROI) programme, which according to the SROI Network UK website 'is an approach to understanding and managing the impacts of a project, organisation or policy. It is based on stakeholders and puts financial value on the important impacts identified by stakeholders that do not have market values.' For more information, see www.sroi-uk.org/component/option, com_frontpage/Itemid,1/.

6

Exceeding your stretch:
a conclusion

> Rather than just adding blogs and photosharing, libraries should adopt the principles of participation in existing core library technologies such as the catalog. Anything less simply adds stress and stretches scarce resources even further. (Lankes et al., 2007)

Because the deeper a library gets into social networking, the more the evidence may scream 'Run! Take cover!' And that despite a lot of enthusiasm and champions. I think about what DiMaio (2009) said, all the issues for consideration explored by Portsmouth, as well as the solutions developed. And while this book is all about planning and making the case for services that can exploit Web 2.0, there is a sense that one can spend so much time preparing that the service is never launched. In other words, in the end thorough implementation of this technology is a risk, and a risk that cannot totally be eliminated by perfect planning. Sometimes the only thing to do is just to go for it!

Right over the BFW, which brings us back to Kathy Sierra's (2005) exhortation to revolution, and what that can mean for public libraries on the ground.

While it is true that public libraries in recent years have seen their business coopted by more agile rivals on the web, which would lend itself to the recommendation for more radical action, public libraries as county- or state-owned franchises, subject to failing budgets, censorship challenges, decreasing staff levels and the tyranny of geography, are not in the position to change their own corporate work practices drastically, never mind their monolithic brand. Public libraries are constantly under pressure to compete in the digital environment at the same time as they are compelled to stick to business as usual in the traditional manner. It is interesting to note that they are not alone in being divided thus – quite a few businesses, such as clothing stores, newspapers even, are in the position of seeing their traditional ways of doing business, in the form of a physical space or object, falling away as they are facing more and more competition online. Web 2.0 can appear as one more way of highlighting that public libraries are outmoded.

All this is by way of saying that while Kathy Sierra's graph is instructive and challenging in a good way (in fact, I would recommend anyone to go to her blog for inspiration because her concept on design is all about the user experience), and while it is necessary to know what is being achieved commercially via Web 2.0, there just might not be any real choice for public librarians: incremental change is really all that can be effected locally, and if done properly it can help in transforming not just public libraries, but other public services with which they interact. We saw this with Portsmouth, as well as Gateshead Libraries which continues to lend its expertise to other government departments.

However, someone, somewhere is going to have to address this issue of radical change, because not only have communication, information, service delivery and business models changed because of the web, but the web itself is changing. Individual brands are giving way to global brands. The whole concept of free information is being challenged. It is difficult to see where institutions so rooted in place can find a niche in this new communication paradigm that continues to evolve and threaten the relevance of public libraries.

In the beginning, the future

But then I think of all the traffic to library catalogues, the system of interlending, and I wonder, do libraries really have to be everyone's best friend, run all these Facebook, MySpace, Second Life, Twitter accounts, trying to be where the action is, but not ever really being in on the action? If we strip away everything and focus on core library business – books and reading – strip back the website to the catalogue, back to this concept of the catalogue as portal, we may be able to see the service afresh. This seems to me to be the direction Oakville and Darien are taking; it's not library websites that need beefing up, it is the openness and functionality of the catalogue, as the main conduit of library business.

But still the motivation to use all the extra functionality has to be found. And that's where the next step comes in.

Humour me. A while ago, I was looking to purchase a film online, and inevitably I started with Amazon. I found the film I wanted, and when I went to 'cash out', I was offered the option of renting the video. This was the first I had seen of this service (Figure 6.1).

It called to mind a talk I gave a while ago on public libraries in 'ongoing digital climate change', which took a broader look at the public library brand in the digital environment (Berube, 2007). My contention was and is that libraries do not need to develop a brand, rather they have an already strong brand that can and should evolve into something stronger in the digital environment. This, of course, would involve a radical shift as recommended by Sierra – one that would require libraries to break out of a purely local service identity to one that fits the global reach of the digital environment. And do this without eliminating that local service ethic. The service delivery model in this instance is not the much-referred-to Amazon, but the floral delivery services, like Interflora, where customers can go to one site, order flowers, and those flowers will be delivered by a local florist. If we then marry this service of local franchise delivery of an international service to the rental service offered by LOVEFilm on the Amazon site, we go some way to resolving the issues of book delivery and return (Figure 6.2). This is what every library cooperative in the UK considering at-home delivery could not solve. This is the problem presenting itself in a similar way with the universal library card here in Britain, and it's not even home delivery at issue, but deliveries to other libraries. Why can't there be the same thing for public libraries as a uniquely branded service online?

With the business model for LOVEFilm, for a monthly fee customers are able to watch any number of films with no time limit on return and so no late fee attached. A prepaid envelope is supplied for the return of DVDs, and once one set is returned, the next can be requested and delivered (together with the monthly fee, this condition secures timely return). There are various deals with different fees depending upon number and frequency. For example, there are 'unlimited' plans where customers can rent up to three DVDs at a time with no overall limit, or 'light use' plans with limitations on the overall number per month. The site explains how this business and service model works:

> One mail centre instead of hundreds of shops makes us very cost-effective. As does using the Royal Mail, who carry our discs to and from your home using first class delivery. Managing our library

Figure 6.1   Amazon

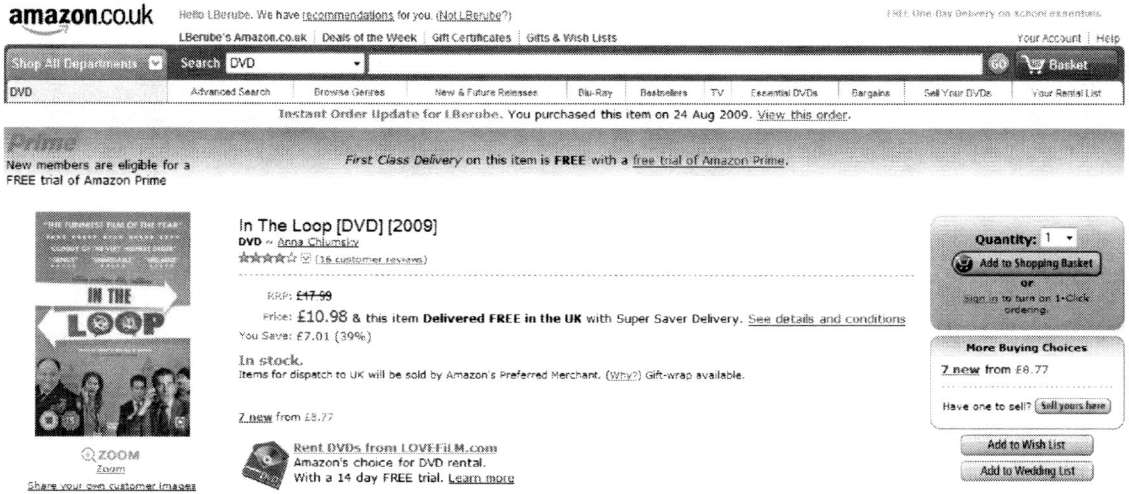

amazon.co.uk

Hello LBerube. We have recommendations for you. (Not LBerube?)

Your Account | Help

FREE One-Day Delivery on school essentials.

LBerube's Amazon.co.uk | Deals of the Week | Gift Certificates | Gifts & Wish Lists

Your Basket | Your Rental List

Shop All Departments

DVD

| Advanced Search | Browse Genres | New & Future Releases | Blu-Ray | Bestsellers | TV | Essential DVDs | Bargains | Sell Your DVDs |

Instant Order Update for LBerube. You purchased this item on 24 Aug 2009. View this order.

First Class Delivery on this item is **FREE** with a free trial of Amazon Prime.

Prime

New members are eligible for a
FREE trial of Amazon Prime

ZOOM
Zoom
Share your own customer images

In The Loop [DVD] [2009]
DVD ~ Armando Iannucci
★★★★☆ (16 customer reviews)

RRP: £17.99
Price: £10.98 & this item **Delivered FREE in the UK** with Super Saver Delivery. See details and conditions
You Save: £7.01 (39%)

In stock.
Items for dispatch to UK will be sold by Amazon's Preferred Merchant. (Why?) Gift-wrap available.

7 new from £8.77

Rent DVDs from LOVEFiLM.com
Amazon's choice for DVD rental.
With a 14 day FREE trial. Learn more

Quantity: 1

Add to Shopping Basket
or
Sign in to turn on 1-Click
ordering.

More Buying Choices

7 new from £8.77

Have one to sell? Sell yours here

Add to Wish List

Add to Wedding List

with the latest technology means we can be very efficient, so we don't need to charge you high prices and late fees.

In Chapter 1 I talked about the much-referenced Amazon model in library circles. In a sense, what librarians are picking up on is the technology – personalisation, referrals within the database environment of searching for and purchasing books. Library catalogue suppliers have noticed this interest and offer the 'mylibrary' functionality for local systems. But in the consideration of social catalogues we saw that all this added personalisation may be fruitless if there is no motivation to participate. The real revitalisation of the library brand is not necessarily found in the technology model; rather it is to be found in the distribution model – the buying and delivery of books without reference to geographic (bookstore) boundaries. So here is a radical concept for

Figure 6.2 LOVEFilm

libraries: where Amazon offers buying the book new or used, there is a third option – to borrow the book from a library. It does not require a rebranding of the library, but rather the next level of evolution or development of the already established brand, a more national/international level that dispenses with geographic boundaries. Of course, there are a few procedural kinks to be worked out: libraries would need to be assured of the return of stock and not only the covering of costs but also perhaps income generation that would help build new and additional stock to cover the requirements of local and national users. In the UK, perhaps regions could pursue the idea of warehouses for stock: in my work in the east of England, at one time, a warehouse for reserve and overflow stock from university, college and public library collections was suggested to resolve space and storage issues. Duplicate stock could be useful for a national borrowing and delivery scheme.

If these conditions can be accomplished, then such a service could be offered through Amazon in the same way as the rental of films – buy the book new, buy the book used, borrow the book. Libraries at once raise the profile of the public library brand, become visible online, and through the building and circulation of stock answer the critics accusing them of abdicating their role with respect to books and reading. Once the interest is rekindled in public libraries and what they can offer to the general public, then adding value to the catalogue, making it more social as in the case of Oakville and Darien, is more attractive as there is more motivation for users not only to contribute to the catalogue but to participate in book clubs, virtual and local.

A stretch too far?

I don't think so, but I am well aware of the logistical, corporate and to a certain extent cultural problems involved in such a concept. But then I see the Canadian initiative with BiblioCommons, where they are trying to build that participation framework at a national level, adding libraries and with them an aggregation of participants already using library catalogues and perhaps motivated enough to submit data. Would ease of delivery added to ease of use supply the motivation for more online communication and participation? It is difficult to say for certain. It would require a great deal of planning and preparation, but in the end, the only thing we can do is take that leap – and hope our communities join us.

References and resources

Unless otherwise noted, all web addresses were accessed and available on 1 November 2010.

References

Alliance Library System (2006) 'Alliance Second Life Library/Info Island announce grand opening', *Alliance Virtual Library*; available at: *http://infoisland.org/2006/10/04/alliance-second-life-libraryinfo-island-announce-grand-opening/*.

American Library Association (2009a) 'ALA releases gaming toolkit', press release; available at: *www.ala.org/ala/newspresscenter/news/pressreleases2009/march2009/olosgamingtoolkit.cfm*.

American Library Association (2009b) 'The librarian's guide to gaming: an online toolkit for building gaming @ your library'; available at: *http://librarygamingtoolkit.org/*.

Arrington, Michael (2009) 'Bloglines on life support. This story needs an ending', *TechCrunch*, 10 August; available at: *www.techcrunch.com/2009/08/10/bloglines-on-life-support-this-story-needs-an-ending/*.

Bejune, Matthew (2007) 'Wikis in libraries', *Information Technology and Libraries*, 26(3): 27–39. See also see companion wiki, now out of date; available at: *http://librarywikis.pbwiki.com/*.

Bell, Lori (2007) 'Info Island brings the Renaissance era to its Second Life!', *NetSquared*, 30 March; available at: *www.netsquared.org/projects/proposals/info-island-brings-renaissance-era-its-second-life*.

Berube, L. (2005) 'E-books in public libraries: a terminal or termination technology?', *Interlending and Document Supply*, 33(1): 14–18.

Berube, L. (2006) 'On the road again: the next e-innovations for public libraries', LASER Foundation report; available at: *www.bl.uk/aboutus/acrossuk/workpub/laser/publications/otherpubs/index.html*.

Berube, L. (2007) 'What do you mean Web 3.0? I just found out about 2.0! Public libraries in ongoing digital library climate change', paper presented at Library 2.0 Forum: Engaging Users and Delivering Innovative Library Services, Library and Information Show, Birmingham, 18 April.

Blyberg, John (2008) 'SOPAC 2.0: what to expect', *Blyberg.net: A Library Geek Blog*, 16 August; available at: *www.blyberg.net/2008/08/16/sopac-20-what-to-expect/*. See also *http://thesocialopac.net/about*.

Booth, A. (2007) 'Blogs, wikis and podcasts: the "evaluation bypass" in action?', *Health Information and Libraries Journal*, 24: 298–302. See also *www.slideshare.net/lisa3859/eblip-library-20-and-australian-health-librarians-revealing-the-evidence*.

Booth, Robert (2009) 'Trafigura: a few tweets and freedom of speech is restored', *The Guardian*, 13 October; available at: *www.guardian.co.uk/media/2009/oct/13/trafigura-tweets-freedom-of-speech*.

Boothe, Ivan (2007) 'Comment in response to "Info Island brings the Renaissance era to its Second Life"', *NetSquared*, 3 April; available at: *www.netsquared.org/projects/proposals/info-island-brings-renaissance-era-its-second-life*. See also Boothe's blog, available at: *www.quixoticlife.net/*.

Bradley, Phil (2007) *How to Use Web 2.0 in Your Library*. London: Facet Publishing.

Camper, Cathy A. (2009) 'Stumptown Comic Fest and Zine Library Group unite', *Graphic Novel Reporter*; available at: *www.graphicnovelreporter.com/content/stumptown-comics-fest-and-zine-library-group-unite-feature-stories*.

Cashmore, Pete (2009) 'YouTube feud ends: U2, Madonna and Green Day videos set to return', *Mashable: The Social Media Guide*, 26 September; available at: *http://mashable.com/2009/09/26/youtube-warner-deal/*.

Chapman, Suzanne (2008) 'University of Michigan main library gateway: library web survey', quoted in DigRef discussion list, 13 January 2008, by Rona Nemer.

Chatfield, Tom (2009) 'Dr Pangloss', *Prospect*, June, p. 13; available at: *www.prospectmagazine.co.uk/2009/06/10806-drpangloss/*.

DiMaio, Andrea (2009) 'Forget a business case for Web 2.0', *Gartner Blog Network*, 28 January; available at: *http://blogs.gartner.com/andrea_dimaio/2009/01/28/forget-a-business-case-for-web-20/*.

Everall, A., Matheson, L., Ormes, S.L. and Williams, D. (2001) 'Stories from the Web: project report', Library and Information Commission Research Report 77; available at: *www.ukoln.ac.uk/public/papers/*.

Fichter, Darlene (2006) 'Web 2.0, Library 2.0 and radical trust: a first take', 2 April; available at: *http://library2.usask.ca/~fichter/blog_on_the_side/2006/04/web-2.html*. See also homepage; available at: *http://library2.usask.ca/~fichter/ index.html*.

Fichter, Darlene (2007a) 'Reviewing Kathy Sierra's "Incremental vs. revolutionary improvements"'; available at: *http://librarywebhead. blogspot.com/2007/04/web-managers-academy-overview-cil2007.html*.

Fichter, Darlene (2007b) 'Radical trust – we're not doing it enough yet', *Blog on the Side*, 20 April; available at: *http://library2. usask.ca/~fichter/blog_on_the_side/2007/04/radical-trust-were-not-doing-it-enough.html*.

Gillmor, Steve (2009) 'Rest in peace, RSS', *TechCrunch*, 5 May; available at: *www.techcrunchit.com/2009/05/05/rest-in-peace-rss/*.

Greenfield, Susan (2009) 'Social websites harm children's brains: chilling warning to parents from top neuroscientist', *Daily Mail Online*, 24 February; available at: *www.tinyurl.com/ckxpap*, quoted in *Library and Information Update*, April, p. 9.

Heil, Bill and Piskorski, Mikolaj (2009) 'New Twitter research: men follow men and nobody tweets', *Harvard Business Publishing*, June; available at: *http://blogs.harvardbusiness.org/cs/2009/06/new_twitter_research_men_follo.html*.

Irvine, Martha (2009) 'Grudgingly, young people finally flock to Twitter', Associated Press, 21 October; available at: *www.thefreelibrary.com/Grudgingly,+young+people+finally+flock+to+Twitter-a01612032958*.

Jefferson, Beth (2007) 'On BiblioCommons', paper presented at Digital Odyssey Conference, Toronto. Information taken from notes by Hyun-Duck Chung on the talk, 21 April; available at: *http:// odyssey2007.wordpress.com/2007/04/21/beth-jefferson-on-the-bibliocommons/*.

Jefferson, Beth (2009) 'Library 2.0 Gang 08/09: social OPACs', podcast, interview hosted by Richard Wallis, *Talis*, 24 August; available at: *http://librarygang.talis.com/2009/08/04/library-20-gang-0809-social-opacs/*. This session also included discussion with John Blyberg.

Keen, Andrew (2007) *The Cult of the Amateur: How Today's Internet Is Killing Our Culture and Assaulting Our Economy*. London: Nicholas Brealey Publishing.

Lamont, Ian (2009) 'Interview with Second Life creator Philip Rosedale', *The Standard*, 30 January; available at: *http://m.thestandard.com/news/2009/01/30/interview-second-life-creator-philip-rosedale?page=0%252C1%2C6* (accessed: 21 October 2009).

Lankes, R. David, Silverstein, Joanne and Nicholson, Scott (2007) 'Participatory networks: libraries as conversation', paper presented at American Library Association's Washington Office via Second Life, February; available at: *http://quartz.syr.edu/rdlankes/presentations/2007/Lankes-SL.mp4*; *http://quartz.syr.edu/rdlankes/presentations/2007/transcript.txt*, reported in ALA District Dispatch; available at: *www.wo.ala.org/districtdispatch/?p= 195.*

Leadbeater, Charles (undated) 'History of Web 2.0: an overview'; available at: *www.charlesleadbeater.net/cms/xstandard/Web2.0_OVerview.pdf.*

Levine, Jenny (2009) 'An open letter to [libraries] on Twitter', *Shifted Librarian*, 5 January; available at: *http://theshiftedlibrarian.com/archives/2009/01/05/an-open-letter-to-libraries-on-twitter.html*, quoted from 'Nina Simon in an open letter to museums on Twitter', *Museum 2.0*, 30 December 2008; available at: *http://museumtwo.blogspot.com/2008/12/open-letter-to-museums-on-twitter.html.*

Lietzau, Zeth (2008) 'U.S. public libraries and Web 2.0: what's really happening?', *Computers in Libraries*, 29(9): 6–10.

Matthew Evans Working Group (1997) 'The new library: the People's Network', report commissioned by the Library and Information Commission and the Department for Culture, Media, and Sport; available at: *www.ukoln.ac.uk/services/lic/newlibrary/.*

McLean, Michelle (2007) 'The connecting librarian', 27 April; available at: *http://connectinglibrarian.com/category/aadl/.*

Miller, Claire Cain (2009) 'Who's driving Twitter popularity? Not teens', *New York Times*, 25 August; available at: *www.nytimes.com/2009/08/26/technology/internet/26twitter.html.*

Morgan Stanley (2009) 'How teenagers consume media', 10 July; available at: *http://media.ft.com/cms/c3852b2e-6f9a-11de-bfc5-00144feabdc0.pdf.*

Nicholson, Scott (2007) 'The role of gaming in libraries: taking the pulse', white paper; available at *http://boardgameswithscott.com/pulse2007.pdf.*

O'Reilly, Tim (2004) 'The architecture of participation', *O'ReillyNet*, June; available at: *www.oreillynet.com/pub/a/oreilly/tim/articles/architecture_of_participation.html.*

O'Reilly, Tim (2005) 'What is Web 2.0: design patterns and business models for the next generation software', *O'ReillyNet*, 30 September; available at: *http://oreilly.com/web2/archive/what-is-web-20.html*.

O'Reilly, Tim (2006) 'Levels of the game: the hierarchy of Web 2.0 applications', *O'Reilly Radar*, 17 July; available at: *http://radar.oreilly.com/archives/2006/07/levels-of-the-game.html*.

OCLC (2007) 'Sharing, privacy and trust in our networked world'; available at: *www.oclc.org/reports/sharing/default.htm*, quoted in *Library and Information Gazette*, 11–24 January 2008, p. 1.

Oder, Norman (2008) 'BiblioCommons emerges: "revolutionary" social discovery system for libraries', *Library Journal*, 18 July; available at: *www.libraryjournal.com/article/CA6579748.html?rssid=191*.

Palos Verdes District Library (2007) 'Director's blog', recording a conversation between library director Kathy Gould and Beth Jefferson of BiblioCommons, 19 November; available at: *http://pvlddirectorsblog.typepad.com/kathy/2007/11/the-catalog---t.html*.

Pavia, Will and Kishtwari, S. (2009) 'Twitter is for old people, work experience whiz kid tells bankers', *Times Online*, 14 July; available at: *www.timesonline.co.uk/tol/news/uk/article6703399.ece*.

Peakdavid (2008) 'Second Life tutorial: beginner's guide – create account & get started in Second Life'; available at: *www.youtube.com/watch?v=2zAb4XxnVMM*.

Pew Internet & American Life Project (2009) 'Twitter and status updating', Fall; available at: *www.pewinternet.org/Reports/2009/17-Twitter-and-Status-Updating-Fall-2009.aspx?r=1*.

Powers, Richard (2002) *Plowing the Dark*. London: Vintage.

Rao, Leena (2009) 'The top 21 Twitter applications (according to Compete)', *TechCrunch*, 19 February; available at: *www.techcrunch.com/2009/02/19/the-top-20-twitter-applications/*.

Rauch, Jonathan (2008) 'Electro-shock therapy', *The Atlantic*, 32(1): 84–95.

Rikomatic (2006) 'Tour of Info Island/Second Life libraries'; available at: *www.youtube.com/watch?v=jTQkzfz5osQ*.

Rochkind, Jonathan (2008) 'Tagging and motivation in library catalogs?', *Bibliographic Wilderness*, 10 May; available at: *http://bibwild.wordpress.com/2008/05/10/tagging-in-library-catalogs/*.

Rogers, E.M. (2003) *Diffusion of Innovations*, 5th edn. New York: Free Press.

Schectman, Joel (2009) 'Iran's Twitter revolution? Maybe not yet', *BusinessWeek*, 17 June; available at: *www.businessweek.com/technology/content/jun2009/tc20090617_803990.htm*.

Shirky, Clay (2007) 'Real Second Life numbers thanks to David Kirkpatrick', *Many2Many*, 4 January; available at: *http://many. corante.com/archives/2007/01/04/real_second_life_numbers_thanks_t o_david_kirkpatrick.php*.

Sierra, Kathy (2005) 'Incremental vs revolutionary improvement', *Creating Passionate Users*, March; available at: *http://headrush. typepad.com/creating_passionate_users/2005/03/incremental_vs_ .html*.

Society of Chief Librarians (2009) 'SCL announces universal membership', 29 September; available at: *www.goscl.com/scl-announces-universal-membership*.

Stephens, Michael (2009) 'SJCPL's "Ray of Light" removed from YouTube', *Tame the Web*, 24 January; available at: *http://tametheweb. com/category/youtube-libraries/*.

Stewart, Ryan (2007) 'Social music overview', *TechCrunch*, 5 February; available at: *www.techcrunch.com/2007/02/05/social-music-overview/*.

Strickland, Jonathan (undated) 'Is there a Web 1.0?', *How Stuff Works*; available at: *http://computer.howstuffworks.com/web-101.htm*.

Thomas, Sarah (2000) 'The catalog as portal to the internet', paper presented at Bicentennial Conference on Bibliographic Control for the New Millennium, Washington, DC, 15–17 November; available at: *www.loc.gov/catdir/bibcontrol/thomas_paper.html*.

West, Jessamyn (2009) 'What happens in a YouTube copyright dispute?', *librarian.net*, 11 January; available at: *www.librarian.net/stax/2653/ what-happens-in-a-copyright-dispute-on-youtube/*.

Westcott, Jezmynne, Chappell, Alexandra and Lebel, Candace (2009) 'LibraryThing for Libraries at Claremont', *Library Hi-Tech*, 27(1): 78–81, special issue on 'Next generation OPACs'; available at: *www.emeraldinsight.com/Insight/viewContainer.do;jsessionid=2FEA2 C887955FDD3EC73AEC4ECA26670?containerType=Issue&contai nerId=15000574*.

Further reading

Bar-Ilan, Judit (2007) 'The use of weblogs (blogs) by librarians and libraries to disseminate information', *Information Research*, 12(4); available at: *http://informationr.net/ir/12-4/paper323.html*.

Bradley, Phil (2009) 'Gathering followers: Twitter in the skies...', *Library and Information Update*, April, pp. 34–7.

Jefferson, Beth (2006) 'Build it – but how to make them come?', paper presented at Digital Odyssey 2006 Conference. Information taken from notes by K. Mogg on the talk, 21 May; available at: *http://odyssey2006.wordpress.com/2006/05/21/build-it-but-how-to-make-them-come/*.

Kiss, Jemima (2007) 'Most teens are MySpacers', *The Guardian*, 17 May; available at: *www.guardian.co.uk/media/2007/may/17/digitalmedia.socialnetworking*.

Quint, Barbara (2007) 'OCLC gets sociable: new social networking initiatives', *Information Today*, 25 June; available at: *http://newsbreaks.infotoday.com/nbReader.asp?ArticleId=36748*.

Rethlefson, Melissa (2007) 'Social bookmarking and tagging boost participation', *Library Journal*, 15 September; available at: *www.libraryjournal.com/article/CA6476403.html*.

Secker, Jane (2008) 'Case study 5: libraries and Facebook', *LASSIE: Libraries and Social Software in Education*, January; available at: *http://clt.lse.ac.uk/Projects/Case_Study_Five_report.pdf*.

Libraries (corporate and/or related Web 2.0 sites)

As is the way with all websites, some of the images taken from library webpages supplied in this publication are no longer available for viewing on the web. However, they have been retained in the text as illustrative of Web 2.0 application and implementation of potential interest to libraries.

Allen Town Public Library: www.youtube.com/watch?v=k3i1OntTcMw

Ann Arbor District Library: www.aadl.org

Ann Arbor Card Catalog Images: www.aadl.org/cat/ccimg/1139602/. Note: Ann Arbor no longer provides a card catalogue image on its page, but does provide the open source software so that other libraries can create a similar service at www.aadl.org/services/devblog/downloads.

Bedfordshire Libraries: www.galaxy.bedfordshire.gov.uk/cgi-bin/vlib.sh; also at Internet Archive's 'Wayback Machine': http://web.archive.org/web/19971012134900/www.earl.org.uk/earl/members/bedfordshire/ or entering the EARL address, www.earl.org.uk, at www.archive.org/web/web.php, selecting the link under 1997 and searching EARL partners.

Cincinnati and Hamilton County Public Library: www.cincinnatilibrary.org/feeds/

Darien Library catalogues SOPAC: www.darienlibrary.org/catalog/record/1245741

Gateshead Arts and Libraries, Children's Book Award: www.asaplive.com/gcba/

Gateshead Arts and Libraries, 'Explore music': www.asaplive.com/ExploreMusic/About.cfm

Gateshead Arts and Libraries, Farne project: www.folknortheast.com

Grand Rapids Public Library, GRPLpedia: www.grpl.org/wiki/index.php/GRPLpedia:About

Hennepin Public Library: www.hclib.org/pub/search/RSS.cfm

Kent County Council Libraries and Archives, libraries and archives discussion forum: http://extranet.kent.gov.uk/cgi-bin/discus/e&l/artslibforum/discus.pl

Lancaster Public Library, 'Get it loud in libraries': www.myspace.com/getitloudinlibraries

McCracken County Library, 'Adventures of super librarian': www.youtube.com/watch?v=Bu-TijjVs_g (some fairly funky comments attached to this video!)

Nashville Public Library start page: www.library.nashville.org/services/ser_computers.asp

Nashville Public Library Teen Web and Delicious pages: www.library.nashville.org/teens/teenweb.asp; www.delicious.com/nashpubya

NorthStarNet: www.northstarnet.org/. Note that the NorthStarNet aggregate calendar, although no longer available on the web, has been retained to illustrate an interesting library-related use of RSS.

Oakville Public Library: www.opl.on.ca/

Oakville Public Library catalogues record: http://opl.bibliocommons.com/item/show/654666001_midnight_for_charlie_bone

Oakville Public Library contest: http://opl.bibliocommons.com/info/contest

Oakville Public Library promotion for contributing to catalogue: http://opl.bibliocommons.com/search?t=title&q=gargoyle

PittCat+: http://pittcatplus.pitt.edu/; for instruction guide: www.library.pitt.edu/guides/pittcatplus/rss.pdf

Portsmouth City Council Library Service, 'The Book Case': www.thebookcase.wetpaint.com

Portsmouth City Council Library Service, 'The Book Case' conditions of use: http://thebookcase.wetpaint.com/page/Conditions+of+Use

Portsmouth City Council Library Service, 'Teen Wiki': http://
teenreadinggroup.wetpaint.com

Princeton Public Library book lovers wiki: http://booklovers.
pbwiki.com/

Scottish Libraries: http://twitter.com/scotlibraries

Sunderland Libraries, 'Their past, your future': www.sunderland.gov.uk/
libraries/theirpastyourfuture.asp

Thomas Ford Memorial Library: www.flickr.com/photos/
thomasfordmemoriallibrary/

Worthingteens: www.myspace.com/worthingteens; www.facebook.com/
worthingteens

Worthingteens blog: http://www2.worthingtonlibraries.org/teen/blog

Worthington Libraries 'Just Read It!': www.youtube.com/watch?
v=lqBl2lV6dEQ

Worthington Libraries 'Thrilled to be Library of the Year': www.
youtube.com/watch?v=jIUa_PenVtI&feature=channel

Web 2.0 tools

Aquabrowser: www.serialssolutions.com/aquabrowser/; www.serials
solutions.com/aquabrowser-my-discoveries; www.librarything.com/
blogs/thingology/2007/08/librarything-and-aquabrowser-my-
discoveries/

BiblioCommons: http://bibliocommons.com

Bloglines: http://bloglines.com

Del.icio.us: http://delicious.com

Drupal: http://drupal.org/ (for UK users see www.drupal.org.uk/)

Facebook: www.facebook.com

Facebook Books weRead: www.facebook.com/BooksweRead

Facebook Bookshare: http://apps.facebook.com/bookshare

feedity: http://feedity.com

Flickr: www.flickr.com/

Furl (now part of Diigo): www.furl.net/root/diigo_info

Google RSS Reader: http://reader.google.com

iGoogle: www.google.com/

Just Tweet It: http://justtweetit.com/education/librarians/

LibraryThing: www.librarything.com/

LibraryThing for Libraries: www.librarything.com/forlibraries/; www.
librarything.com/thingology/2007/08/librarything-and-aquabrowser-
my.php

MySpace: www.myspace.com

MySpace FAQs 'Pop-out your MySpace music player': http://faq.
myspace.com/app/answers/detail/a_id/98

My Yahoo: http://my.yahoo.com

Napster: www.napster.co.uk/

Netvibes: www.netvibes.com/

Overdrive: http://overdrive.com

Pageflakes: www.pageflakes.com/

Podcast Alley: www.podcastalley.com/search.php?searchterm=library

Second Life: http://secondlife.com/

Twellow: www.twellow.com/

TwitPics: http://twitpics.com

Twitter: http://twitter.com/

Twitter Grader: http://twitter.grader.com/

Typepad: www.typepad.com/

WetPaint: www.wetpaint.com/

WikiMatrix: www.wikimatrix.org/

Wordpress: http://wordpress.org/

YouTube: www.youtube.com

Other websites and resources

Amazon search for 'In the Loop' DVD: www.amazon.co.uk/Loop-DVD-
Anna Chlumsky/dp/B002AQQVDC/ref=sr_1_1?ie=UTF8&s=dvd&
qid=1251208835&sr=1-1

American Library Association: www.alatechsource.org/ltr/gaming-and-
libraries-intersection-of-services

Answers.com: www.answers.com/topic/retronym

BiblioCommons, announcement of launch in 2008: http://
theshiftedlibrarian.com/archives/2008/07/23/bibliocommons-goes-
live.html

Fry, Stephen: http://twitter.com/STEPHENFRY ('tweet' referred to in
chapter no longer available)

Howard Rheingold: www.rheingold.com/

Info Island: http://infoisland.org/

Interflora: www.interflora.co.uk/

Internet Archive WayBack Machine: www.archive.org/web/web.php

'Library 2.0', Wikipedia: http://en.wikipedia.org/wiki/Library_2.0

'Library and information science: weblogs', Open Directory Project: http://search.dmoz.org/cgi-bin/search?search=librarians&all=no &cs=UTF-8&cat=Reference%2FLibraries%2FLibrary_and_ Information_Science%2FWeblogs

'Libraries and Web 2.0': http://librariesandweb2.wetpaint.com/

'Library success: a best practices wiki': www.libsuccess.org/index. php?title=Virtual_Worlds

LOVEFilm: www.lovefilm.com/learn/product.html?product_id=128157

'Microblogging', Wikipedia: http://en.wikipedia.org/wiki/Microblogging

People's Network Enquire: www.peoplesnetwork.gov.uk/

Rowanfair, 'SL libraries: Info Island archipelago tour': www.youtube. com/watch?v=B8v3TZethQ0

Rikomatic, 'The click heard round the world': www.rikomatic. com/blog/2006/10/riks_skate_tour.html

SOPAC resources: http://my.opera.com/LibraryImportant/blog/2008/ 09/09/new-open-source-social-catalog-sopac-2-0-debuts-in-darien-public-library; http://blogs.talis.com/panlibus/archives/2008/09/john-blyberg-talks-with-talis-about-sopac-20.php

StoryTubes: www.storytubes.info/

TechCrunch group-edited technology blog: www.techcrunch.com

UKOLN: www.ukoln.ac.uk/about/

University of Calgary podcast wiki: http://wiki.ucalgary.ca/index. php/Podcasting

'Web 1.0', Wikipedia: http://en.wikipedia.org/wiki/Web_1.0

'Web 2.0', Wikipedia: http://en.wikipedia.org/wiki/Web_2.0

'Your chickens: a kids guide': www.youtube.com/watch?v= B9P17eYfp4E

Index

CPSIA information can be obtained at www.ICGtesting.com

261223BV00003B/1/P

9 781843 344360